The Prophetic Worshiper

Heaven's Sounds in the Hearts of a Lovesick Generation

Pablo Pérez

*T*ruth *P*ress

Diffusing the Fragance of the Knowledge of God

Kansas City, Missouri

The Prophetic Worshiper

Copyright © 2004 by Pablo Perez. All rights reserved.

Published by *Truth Press*.

Kansas City, Missouri

Edited by Edie Veach

Printed in the United Sates of America on acid-free paper.
ISBN 1-931600-87-2

Ordering Information

Truth Press
P.O.BOX 17715
Kansas City, MO 64134
www.truthpress.com

"Pablo Perez brings years of experience as a psalmist to this powerful subject. His personal passion for the primacy of Jesus in worship gives this book prophetic focus. I believe this book will be a tool to train young worship leaders in many cultures and nations."

Bob Sorge
Author of *"Exploring Worship"*

"I have known and worked with Pablo for some years. I believe that the Lord has placed a message in his heart for this generation. The music of God's presence will invade our worship gatherings and lead us to behold the glory of the Man Christ Jesus."

Mike Bickle
Director of the International
House of Prayer of Kansas City.

"Pablo Perez is a young lion of praise who understands kingdom reality concerning musicians, music and worship. Those realties of brokenness, humility, holiness, intimacy and sacrifice which few musicians understand and practice are keys to the supernatural music of God's presence. *"The Prophetic Worshiper"* will help you see those realities and wet your appetite to pursue them. I recommend this book."

LaMar Boschman
Dean of The Worship Institute
Dallas, TX

"Worship has always been and always will be *the issue* of the ages. The question that has to be answered by everyone is this: To whom will we give our allegiance and affections? In this pointed and inspirational book, Pablo challenges us to personally answer this question as he passionately calls us to embrace the heart of true worship. I highly recommend this book."

S. J. Hill
Bible teacher and
Author of *"Enjoying God"*

"Pablo Perez's book is "must reading" for every worship leader. Sharing from his own personal passion for deeper levels of intimacy with God, Pablo targets key issues to stir the heart and soul of musician worshippers. There is a new sound coming forth from the realm of the Spirit. It is revolutionizing music as we know it and is irresistible to those who are aggressively chasing after God. *"The Prophetic Worshiper"* is written to open the door for greater understanding of the outpouring of the Glory of God. With refreshing insight on familiar scriptural passages, Pablo lays a firm foundation by advancing a proper understanding of true worship. Then he leads the reader on a journey of self-examination while increasing personal hunger for God. Each chapter ends with a recap of important points for further meditation. My wife and I have had the privilege of knowing Pablo on and off the stage. More than a gifted musician, Pablo's leadership emerges from a heart broken before God and a genuine hunger to see God's people discover the Music of His Presence.

Pastor Phil Derstine
Christian Retreat Family Church
President, Gospel Crusade International

"Pablo Perez is a truly anointed musician who has been touched by God to bring forth this book. His insights will help many to tap into the sounds of heaven. The truths that he brings forth will open hearts and minds to passionately pursue a deeper intimacy with our Lord and to become vessels that pour forth living waters. It has been my joy to know Pablo as a friend and fellow minister. When I first heard his music I recognized the heavenly sound and was overjoyed. The combination of skill and anointing truly bring glory to God! I believe this book to be one of the tools that will be used as we are watching the restoration of David's Tabernacle take place in these days."

Rev. Janet Shell

Dedication

I dedicate this book to the One who intercepted my journey years ago and has since revolutionized my life. He is the unrelenting Pursuer of my soul — the precious, tenacious, patient, and ever-loving Holy Spirit.

Contents

Introduction

More than a decade ago, I was part of a worship team. I played the piano in services and sang on occasion. I realized that my music did not have life. It was only an expression of the technique, hollow and empty.

I couldn't stand this situation any longer, so I went to a man of God and said: *"I feel empty and dry. My music does not transmit life, only death. I can't stand being like this anymore and don't want to play just to play and sing just to sing. I desire the Holy Spirit to flow through me. What should I do so that the life of God floods my being and is reflected in my music?"*

I have never forgotten the answer that this man gave me. He said: *"The only way to transmit life is to find it. You have to have a personal and true encounter with Jesus because He is the life. Then, in the measure that you abide in Him and develop an intimate relationship with God, your music will reflect His life, and it won't be empty and dead anymore."*

I was worried about the music but needed God in my whole being. I couldn't separate one thing from the other. If there was going to be life in the music, it would be because life was coming from the depth of my heart.

When I was a kid, my parents did their best to instruct me in the ways of God. However, one day I realized that though I had lots of information about Jesus Christ, I had no personal encounter with Him. This brought me to seek Him like never before. As I sought Him more and more, my desire for Him increased. This search went on until one day something marvelous happened. Honestly, I cannot tell you what I found, except that He found me. Since then, I have been getting to know Him more and more. One thing I have come to understand in this time is— an anointed worshiper

1

is the result of a continuous, deep, and personal relationship with the Lord Jesus Christ. Intimacy with Jesus is the key to flow in the anointing and to minister life.

In our days, the Holy Spirit is raising a multicultural generation of prophetic worshipers. He is fascinating them with the beauty and the majesty of the Man Christ Jesus. They are coming to know the Lord as He really is and their hearts and affections are burning with holy passion. They are growing in confidence, knowing that they are loved and desired by the uncreated God. They will be a lovesick company of people that walks in the fullness of God— *the fullness of His power and the fullness of His nature.* They will bring forth the sound from heaven and prepare the way for the King of glory to return and establish His kingdom on earth.

I offer this book as a contribution for this generation of worshipers. I am convinced that the reader will find treasures of wisdom and revelation throughout the pages of this work. Each chapter shares a portion of what the Lord has graciously showed me through the years. Subjects like— *The Music of His Presence. Learning to follow the Holy Spirit during corporate gatherings. Intimacy with Jesus. Releasing the sound from heaven. Walking in holiness and integrity. Prayer and fasting. Etc.* I also deal with some of the destructive ways of the human character. Dimensions of darkness and hypocrisy are exposed and confronted, which may be found offensive and disruptive for some. *But* if you manage not to get tangled in the thorns that pierce your soul, *you will arrive at the rose of this book,* and your heart will grow in the knowledge of God.

Chapter 1

The Music of His Presence

A new sound is coming to the earth. It will be very powerful, like nothing we have heard or experienced before. One of the components of that new sound is what I like to call — *the Music of His Presence.*

It is music that has been born in the heart of God. Like a torrent of freedom and power that descends from on high and changes everything in its path, something very difficult to describe with words, but yet very real. It is music full of the majesty and the glory of God.

I firmly believe that the music of His presence will be one of the distinguishing characteristics of the Church of the end times. It will completely revolutionize our worship services and will carry us to behold the very glory of the King. The music of His presence flows from the realm of God's glory. It's a combination of melodies and harmonies that come from the throne room of heaven and break into the earth realm. As we will see, this heavenly sound flows through a growing generation of prophetic worshipers. They are an army of lovesick singers and musicians that will hear, taste and become the sound from heaven.

Since this generation of prophetic worshipers has such an important calling, it's essential for them to experientially know the realm of God's glory.

The Cloud of God's Presence

Let's briefly look to the life of Moses — he had continuous access to the glory realm.

> As he went into the tent, the pillar of cloud would come down and hover at the entrance while the Lord spoke with Moses ....*the Lord would speak to Moses face to face, as a man speaks to his friend (Ex. 33:9-11, NLT).*

Moses' relationship with God was so intimate that he became His companion and friend. The Lord could speak face to face with Moses without impediments or obstacles. It was a remarkable and amazing relationship that existed between the two of them.

On one occasion, God said to him:

> "...Come up to Me on the mountain and be there; and I will give you....Then Moses went up into the mountain, and a cloud covered the mountain... Now the glory of the Lord rested on Mount Sinai, and the cloud covered it six days. And on the seventh day He called to Moses out of the midst of the cloud" (Ex. 24: 12, 15, 16).

When Moses went up to Sinai, a cloud covered the mount, and the glory of the Lord rested there for six days. This was a powerful experience. Nevertheless, Moses continued waiting, obeying the voice of Him who had told him, *"stay there; and I will give you"*. During those six days the Holy Spirit covered Moses, and he felt the glory of God that rested on the mount, but there was more. On the seventh day, while he was in the midst of the cloud, the Lord called him again. This call was distinct and much more intense.

> The sight of the glory of the Lord was like a consuming fire on the top of the mountain in the eyes of the children of Israel. So Moses went into the midst of the cloud and went up into the mountain. And Moses was on the mountain forty days and forty nights (*Ex. 24:17-18*).

Moses could climb up the mount to a certain point, but in order to climb higher, he had to listen to the call of God and enter in the midst of the cloud. When Moses entered the cloud, *he entered into the Spirit*. It was no longer Moses that climbed. *The Holy Spirit carried him*. He had crossed the threshold of the door that divides the natural from the supernatural, and entered into the spiritual realm. The Lord showed him eternal things, things that are not seen in the natural. It was there where he had the revelation of the tabernacle and many other types and shadows of things to come.

Moses' life and his ministry were radically changed. He had experienced the tremendous power that flowed from his staff. He was an eyewitness of the extraordinary miracles done by God. After entering the cloud, however, a cry rose up in his heart: *'show me now Your way, that I may know You'* (*Ex. 33:13*).

Entering the realm of the Spirit did not only open a new world of revelation for Moses, it also produced a fervent desire deep inside of him to know the nature and personality of God more than anything else.

The music of His Presence is found in this realm of the Spirit. Finding this realm will not only be impressive and revealing, but it will also produce the same longing in you that was produced in Moses, *a passionate desire to know the Lord more deeply*.

The music of His Presence is more real than you can imagine, just like the realm of the Spirit. The fact that someone

may not know this realm does not mean that it doesn't exist.
Like I said before — *It is not just the music of men to God but
from God to men.* It is found in Him, and it flows from His
very being.

The Realm of the Spirit

*Thus says the Lord, who makes a way in the sea and a path
through the mighty waters (Is. 43:16).* The children of Israel never
imagined that they were going to pass through the depths of
the sea. For them there was no way; they
thought that they were going to die *(Ex. 14:11),* but God
opened a way in the sea. He carried them in a way that was
logically and reasonably impossible. It was a way that the
human mind could not comprehend because its dimension
was divine, not human.

The Holy Spirit removed the Israelites from the material
realm, where they moved in the five senses, and introduced
them to a spiritual realm in which everything was possible.
This realm was a supernatural world in which they could
only enter by faith. This was the unknown for them, but as I
said before — *the fact that it was unknown to them did not mean
that it didn't exist.*

The Door to the Realm of the Spirit

There is a door that separates the natural realm from the
realm of the Spirit. This door was very real for the apostle
John:

Then as I looked, *I saw a door* standing open in
heaven... The voice said, "Come up here, and I will show
you... And *instantly I was in the Spirit....* (Rev. 4:1- 2 NLT).

John looked and saw an open door in the heavens, and a voice said unto him, *come up here.* In other words, the Lord was saying, *"Down there you are not going to be able to see anything, you need to come up here; you have to pass through the door and enter into My world."*

This was new to John. Despite the fact that in the past he had heard the voice of the Lord say, *'I am the door...' (Jn. 10:9),* he was finally beginning to understand the magnitude of what the Master had said. When John passed through the door, he left the world of reason and entered *the world of the Spirit.* He left the natural in order to enter the supernatural. *"And instantly I was in the Spirit..."* In the twinkling of an eye, John found himself before the throne of God, and he beheld the worship of heaven.

Was this experience just for John? Of course not. There are other people in the Bible who experienced it. Days present and past testify to this. Is it possible for a musician or singer to pass through this door and enter in the Spirit? Yes! Absolutely!

My Personal Experience

What I am about to share is my experience with the *music of His Presence.* My experience is not all that there is. In fact, it is just the tip of the iceberg.

The following words should be received as a testimony, not as doctrine or law. Our God is creative and does with each person as He desires. His principles do not change, but His forms and methods of acting vary every day. You will not find the *music of His Presence* trying to imitate a particular experience, but rather by encountering the *Fountain*—God.

It is not easy to describe it, but while I am ministering to the Lord with the piano (*during a service or in my personal devotions*), there are moments in which He opens a door in the realm of the Spirit and invites me to come up. Upon passing through the door, I enter in the Spirit. *In that instant, it is no longer I following Him, but rather He carries me.* The harmony and the melody begin to flow with an indescribable freshness — unmistakably too difficult to express. It is like a powerful river of which I am in the middle and its current takes me wherever it wants. It is like extending my wings and flying impulsively on the wind without limits or pressure, in absolute and perfect liberty.

The Scriptures declares, *"Those who wait upon the Lord will rise up wings like eagles."(Is.40:31).*This bird extends its wings and surrenders itself to the power of the wind at the great heights, where the air currents are very strong. The eagle only moves its wings to reach the level of the current, but when it gets there, it extends its wings and allows the wind to propel it along. In this way, the eagle arrives to heights and velocities that it could not reach on its own. Although this is difficult to illustrate, something similar occurs in the realm of the Spirit. I can extend my wings and surrender myself to the wind of the Holy Spirit without any effort because it is He who moves me. In doing so, the harmony reaches its highest heights, and then slowly descending, penetrates the heart in a most profound way. After descending, many times the music will begin to intensify (*in crescendo*) again, gaining more strength and power in proportion to the increase of the Spirit. It is as if the Spirit (*above all, in services of corporate worship*) wraps up all those present in His wings, lifting them to new heights of the glory of God. The music becomes inexpressible, powerful, majestic, and glorious.

At other times, it is as if the *Cloud* rests upon a chord, giving it sharpness and depth and bringing a holy silence to the place. Then He begins to descend like sweet dew, full of the majesty of God.

"I will be as the dew unto Israel: he shall grow as the lily, and cast forth his roots as Lebanon" *(Hosea 14:5, KJV).*
"It is like the dew of Hermon, descending upon the mountains of Zion; for there the Lord commanded the blessing—life forevermore" *(Ps. 133:3).*

Then, the freshness of the Presence of God floods the congregation of the saints, and everything that was dry is renewed. The music flows and tenderizes the hearts of the people, preparing the ground so that the seed of life will fall on good earth. As the book of Numbers declares:

'And when the dew fell on the camp in the night, the manna fell on it' (Num. 11:9). When the dew of His presence drenches the human heart, then it is ready to receive divine nourishment— *the Word of God.*

The music of His Presence finds different expressions with every prophetic worshiper. What I've shared it's just the testimony of my own experience—which is just a drop of a big ocean. It takes all of us to express the fullness and richness of this heavenly sound.

One in the Spirit

The union between the leader (lead worshiper, prayer leader, pastor etc.) and the musicians is one of the dynamics of the music of His Presence. Both flow in the same direction as if they were bound together. Sometimes there isn't even an exchange of words because they are both inspired by the same Spirit, *the Spirit of God.*

That day David first committed to Asaph and his associates this psalm of thanks to the Lord.... *(1 Chr. 16:7, NIV).*

It was David, Asaph and associates. There was a spiritual bond that existed between them. They went in the same direction and arrived together at the same goal because the same Spirit guided them. So that this becomes possible, both the leader and the musicians need to be guided by the Holy Spirit, and both need to know the realm of the Spirit. It is necessary for them to be one; because if there is not unity, neither will there be coordination, and one of the two leaders will end up frustrated. The leader and the musicians should seek this unity, the spontaneity and creativity of the music of His Presence requires it. When the preacher and the musicians flow in the same Spirit, the intensity of the Word of God is powerfully backed up by the music. This becomes a stamp of the divine message. Each truth is accentuated and harmonized by a heavenly touch.

The unity of the Spirit between the one who leads and the musicians is a very powerful weapon, and we should learn to use it.

The Song of the Beloved

To end this chapter, I would like to brieflly highlight one of the most powerful dimensions of the music of His Presence—the song of the beloved.

There is a song that our Heavenly Bridegroom sings. As the prophet Isaiah said:

Let me (as God's representative) *sing of and for* my greatly Beloved (God, the Son) *a tender song of my Beloved* concerning His vineyard (His chosen people)" (*Is. 5:1 Amp*).

God is the creator of music, and He is the best musician and singer in the entire universe. The music of His presence carries the passion of the Bridegroom's heart for His bride. It is an expression of the ravished heart of God — a manifestation of His intense desire.

The book of Song of Songs, *the most excellent song ever written*, portrays King Jesus singing out His burning desire for us:

> "How beautiful you are, my darling, Oh, how beautiful!" (*S.g.4:1, NIV*).
>
> "You have ravished my heart, my sister, my spouse; you have ravished my heart with one look of your eyes" (*S.g.4:9*).

Oh! To hear the music and the song of the unconditional lover of our souls — it's a life changing experience! There is nothing like it!

The music of His presence is an expression of the deep and strong affection that *Christ* has for His *people*. His sweetness and majesty are indescribable. They are a live reflection of the passionate heart of our amazing God.

Conclusion

Dear reader, the music of His presence is part of your glories inheritance. Right now there is a door standing open before you, a portal of light that leads to the throne room — the realm of God's glory and beauty. It's time to engage this revelatory realm. It's time to go up in worship. Hear His voice calling you, wooing you to ascend, saying — *"Come up Here, and I will show you...."*

- To Meditate -

✓ A new sound is coming to the earth, one that I have considered calling in a personal manner — *the Music of His Presence.*

✓ The music of His Presence will be one of the distinguishing characteristics that the Church of the last days will have. It will completely revolutionize our worship services and will carry us to behold the very glory of the King.

✓ The music of His presence flows from the realm of God's glory. It's a combination of melodies and harmonies that come from the throne room of heaven and break into the earth realm.

✓ This music is like a powerful river of which you are in the middle and its current takes you wherever it wants. It is like extending your wings and flying impulsively on the wind without limits or pressure, in absolute and perfect liberty.

✓ The music of His presence carries the passion of the Bridegroom's heart for His bride. It is an expression of His ravished heart — a manifestation of His intense desire.

Chapter 2

Learning to Follow Him

The Lord went ahead of them in a pillar of cloud *to guide them on their way (Ex. 13:21, NIV).*

During the exodus of the people of Israel, God guided them on their path. The people of Israel did not go in the direction that they wanted; they followed the way that God marked out for them with the cloud.

In each worship service, when we lead the people into the Presence of God, we have to discern which direction the cloud is going and follow it. Sadly, the custom of taking our own paths and following only what we have programmed makes it difficult for us to see the path that the Spirit wants to guide us along. We need to observe where the cloud is going and follow it. The way that the Spirit leads us along is different every time. The path is not the same from one day to the next, and the direction that worked yesterday will not necessarily be the one that works today. *(In this chapter, the use of the word "Way" or "Path" will be in reference to a specific direction given by the Holy Spirit, before or during the service).*

If we search the Scriptures well, we will find that the cloud that guided the Israelites in the wilderness was not *something,* but rather *someone.*

17

Where is the one who brought Israel through the sea, with
Moses as their shepherd? Where is the one *who sent his Holy
Spirit to be among* his people? ....As with cattle going down
into a peaceful valley, the Spirit of the Lord gave them rest.
You led your people, Lord *(Is. 63:11–14, NLT).*

By saying, *"who sent his Holy Spirit to be among his people"*
and *"the Spirit of the Lord gave them rest. You led your people,
Lord…"* the prophet Isaiah points that the cloud that guided
the people was a representation, or a symbol, of the Holy
Spirit. He is the one who guides us and makes us walk in the
paths that we have not known before, paths that are full of
life and glory that transform and revolutionize our
preconceptions about worship.

Moving With the Cloud

The people of Israel moved when the cloud moved.
When it rested in a place, they also rested there until it moved
again.

When *the cloud lifted* from over the sacred tent, *the people of
Israel followed it.* And wherever the cloud settled, the people
of Israel camped. In this way, they traveled *at the Lord's
command* and stopped wherever he told them to" *(Num. 9:17-
18, NLT. See also Ex. 40:36-37).*

They had to daily observe the cloud because they never
knew when it would change direction. They were in the desert
and didn't know the way. The people depended on the cloud
to keep them from getting lost or taking the wrong path.

The book of Numbers declares: *"they traveled at the Lord's
command."* God used the cloud to inform the Israelites when

they should move, in what direction, and when to stop.

We need to be sensitive to the Holy Spirit. He desires to lead us and tenderize our hearts. If we give Him place in our lives and complete liberty in the services, He will show us the way. The Spirit knows everything. He knows exactly what His people need. If we submit to Him and follow Him, He will give us the right songs and words. As Isaiah declares:

> Your ears shall hear a word behind you, saying, 'This is the way, walk in it,' Whenever you turn to the right hand or whenever you turn to the left (*Is. 30:21*).

We find another example of this on the book of Ezekiel. When the prophet had the vision of the glory of the Lord, he saw the cherubs and the form that they moved in. *"Each one went straight ahead. Wherever the spirit would go, they would go, without turning as they went." (Ez.1:12, NIV).* The phrase *"Wherever the spirit would go, they would go"* indicates a total dependence upon God.

Jesus said: *'I tell you the truth, the Son can do nothing by himself; he can do only what he sees his Father doing, because whatever the Father does the Son also does' (Jn. 5:19, NIV).* He needed to see and hear what the Father was doing in order to move. He didn't move by His own will. He was continually connected to the Father to see what He desired. *He moved according to that which He saw.* Now, if Jesus Christ couldn't do anything by Himself, how much more are we not able to do anything by ourselves?

We need to develop an intimate relationship with God. Then, we will learn to follow Him. When we are in His presence, our heart becomes sensitive and our dependence on the Holy Spirit grows.

A Blind Man Reached By Grace

In order to follow someone, you must first see him; if you don't see the person, you will not be able to see the path he takes.

A few years back, I found myself in services and heard the pastor say, *"God is here,"* or *"You can feel His presence in this place"*. I asked myself, *"How does he know? Why does he perceive it and I don't?*

The fact that others perceived the Presence of God and I wasn't even aware of it made me desperate. At that time, I could only recognize God's Presence in a place because someone told me that it was there or because I saw His glory reflected in the faces of the people, but I couldn't realize it for myself. My heart was hard, and my spiritual eyes were closed. I was blind! It was not easy to accept that fact. Nevertheless, it was my first step towards the light.

Many times I felt I identified with Job: *'If He goes by me, I do not see Him; If He moves past, I do not perceive Him' (Job 9:11).* He passed before me, and I did not see Him. Others saw Him and recognized His Presence, but not I. This all resulted in a prayer being born in my heart: *'God, I want to know you!'* Although I am a preacher's kid and had heard the Bible since I can remember, I had only acquired information about God, but I did not know Him personally. This prayer transformed into a cry, a profound thirst, and a hunger to find Him whom I did not know. For some time there was no answer, and His silence seemed to augment my darkness, but one day His grace reached me, and a glimmer of light entered my soul.

"Then I will give them one heart, and I will put a new spirit within them, and take the stony heart out of their flesh, and give them a heart of flesh" (Ez. 11:19).

'Then I will give them a heart to know Me, that I am the Lord... they shall be My people, and I will be their God, for they shall return to Me with their whole heart' (Jer. 24:7).

I can remember the sweet voice of the Holy Spirit saying to me: *"Starting today, I am taking out your heart of stone and I am putting in a heart that is tender and sensitive to My Presence. You will feel My power flowing through you and you will know when I am being revealed among My people."*

Since that day, every time He comes close, my heart burns with passion. Little by little I could perceive in my spirit when His cloud moves among the people. After missing His direction many times, His course is clearer every day.

God promises to guide the blind along paths that they do not know and to go before them to change their darkness to light. I can testify of His love and His mercy because He did not abandon me in the darkness. Perhaps, I have not been able to explain myself very well, but *'One thing I do know. I was blind but now I see'* (Jn. 9:25, NIV).

Now, I would like to end this chapter bringing some balance and further understanding concerning following the direction of the Spirit in a service. Like I declared before, many times I have made mistakes in an attempt to follow His direction, thinking that He was going *"south"* and finding out later that He was going *"north."* You know what? Knowing myself, there are countless chances of future mistakes. But I have found a truth that has freed my soul – *Jesus is not intolerant like some men.* He tolerates mistakes. Yes! If you are not convinced of this, I invite you to study the life of the disciples. You will be amazed and shocked when you discover to whom Jesus gave the keys of the kingdom of Heaven. *He did not take them back when this person severely failed.* As long as you have a willing spirit and readiness to learn, don't be afraid of getting it wrong. *Be sure of this* – eventually you will make mistakes trying to follow His direction in a service! So, don't get discouraged when it happens. Learn from your mistakes and keep following Him. Throw away and refuse all religious tension. Get rid of all condemnation and insecurity caused by past failures, resist the *Accuser,* have plain confidence in Jesus who deeply loves you, and trust in his Holy Spirit who is eager to help you. *On the contrary,* you will be afraid to move – scared – enslaved by fear – lacking initiative – completely intimidated and hesitant.

Trust the Lord and be encouraged! Like Paul prayed:

"May our Lord Jesus Christ himself and God our father, *who loved us and by his* grace gave us eternal encouragement and good hope, encourage your hearts and strengthen you in every good deed and word" (*2 Thes. 2:16-17 NIV*).

Hallelujah! Don't give up! Don't lose your willingness to learn! Rejoice always in God who promises to make you understand and instructs you in the way you should go. He keeps saying:

I will instruct you and teach you in the way you should go;
I will guide you with My eye (*Ps. 32:8*).

- To Meditate -

✓ Jesus needed to see and hear what the Father was doing in order to move. He didn't move by His own will. He was continually connected to the Father to see what He desired. *He moved according to that which He saw.* Now, if Jesus Christ couldn't do anything by Himself, how much more are we not able to do anything by ourselves?

✓ As long as you have a willing spirit and readiness to learn, don't be afraid of getting it wrong. Be sure of this – *Eventually you will make mistakes trying to follow His direction in a service*! So, don't get discouraged when it happens; learn from your mistakes and keep following Him.

✓ Throw away and refuse all religious tension; get rid of all condemnation and insecurity. Have plain confidence in Jesus who loves you and in his Holy Spirit who is eager to help you.

✓ We need to develop an intimate relationship with God, and then we will learn to follow Him. When we are in His Presence our heart becomes sensitive, and our dependence on His Spirit grows.

Chapter 3

Transmitting His Reality

Have you ever observed how a radio receptor works? Isn't it interesting? The antenna receives radio waves that are in the air and communicates them through a simple speaker. When you turn the radio *on* you hear two things: *voices and music.* Now, in order to hear the broadcast from these waves, the radio receptor needs to be turned on and the antenna up. If the radio is turned off, it will not emit any sound, and if it is turned on, but the antenna is down, the sound will be vague and fuzzy. The two conditions need to be met in order to have the radio function properly. And besides all that, there are different frequencies, and one needs to know how to tune in to the correct station.

Allow me to take this and compare it to spiritual things. The radio receptor is *our heart*, and the antenna is our spiritual perception. The dial is the capacity to tune in to the frequency of the Spirit, and the speaker is our mouth and/or our hands that communicate His voice and transmit His music. Considering this, we can ask ourselves: *Are our hearts on fire and open to perceive the signal of the Spirit, or are they turned off? Do we keep the antenna up high, or do we only raise it when necessary? What frequency are we generally tuned in to and what do we transmit?*

It is time to be like the receptor that is turned on and has its antenna high in the air. The frequency of the Spirit of God is real, and there are sounds and words found there.

A prophetic worshiper is someone that communicates the reality God's presence. This reality affects the atmosphere of a place and is sensed and perceived for those who are present.

As I said before, prophetic worshipers come to experientially know the glory realm. Then, from that place of revelation they are able to transmit God's sounds and words. We find a great example of this in the life of the prophet Ezekiel. He knew the realm of the Spirit and developed a very sharp sensitivity to the supernatural.

> Then the Spirit took me up and brought me in a vision by the Spirit of God...." *Ez. 11:24*
>
> He stretched out the form of a hand, and took me by a lock of my hair; and the Spirit lifted me up between earth and heaven, and brought me in visions of God...(*Ez. 8:3*).

Ezekiel was literally taken and carried by the Spirit in visions. Some of the things he saw revealed the degrading condition of the people. Others spoke of God's future plans for them, and still others, of the glory and holiness of God. Why did the Holy Spirit share these things? We find the reason at the beginning of his ministry.

> Son of man, I have made you a watchman for the house of Israel; therefore hear a word from My mouth, and give them warning from Me:... Hear what I say to you... open your mouth and eat what I give you...Then He said to me: "Son of man, go to the house of Israel and speak with My words to them." (Ez. 3:17; 2:8; 3:4).

Ezekiel's call was to be a watchman for Israel. He was to report to the people all that he heard and saw in the spiritual realm. He was a communicator of the divine Word. He did not speak his own words nor transmit a dead form from the past. He spoke what he heard. *He was the voice of God for his generation.*

Communicating His Voice

We find another example in the time of King Jehoshaphat. There was a Levite of the sons of Asaph who prophesied to the whole kingdom of Judah.

> ...*the Spirit of the Lord came upon one of the men*... His name was Jahaziel son of Zechariah... *a Levite who was descendant of Asaph*. He said, 'Listen, all you people of Judah and Jerusalem! This is what the Lord says: Do not be afraid! Don't be discouraged by this mighty army, for the battle is not yours, but God's' (*2 Chr. 20:14-15, NLT*).

Jahaziel was connected with God, and when the moment arrived, the Spirit came over him and he prophesied to the people. The Lord looks for Levites that are connected to Him, musicians that not only play or sing, but also perceive the message of the heart of God.

We should be transmitters of the *signal* of heaven, not just *"echoes"* of what we hear other men say. It is good and necessary to receive from the servants of God, but if we solely depend on those who transmit His Spirit and never seek to personally hear His voice, we will become religious parrots that only know how to repeat but have not learned to receive directly from the Lord. Besides, a copy, no matter how good it is, will never have the quality of the original.

Transmitting His Reality

Prophetic worshipers present a real and living God, not a remote story about Him. They flow in the anointing of the Holy Spirit and portray a fresh revelation of Jesus.

> That which was from the beginning, which we have heard, which we have seen with our eyes, which we have looked upon, and our hands have handled, concerning the Word of life—the life was manifested, and we have seen, and bear witness, and declare to you that eternal life...was manifested to us.... (1 Jn. 1:1-2).

John announced to man what he had heard, seen, gazed at, and touched of the *Son of God*. He gave testimony of a reality because the Word of life had been manifested to him. We can also observe this in the life of the apostle Paul. When Jesus appeared to him on the road to Damascus, He said: '...*for I have appeared to you for this purpose, to make you a **minister and a witness** both of the things which you have seen and of the things which I will yet reveal to you'*(Acts 26:16). Paul was a minister and a witness. He proclaimed what he had seen of Jesus. He did not teach with human wisdom, rather he transmitted what he received from the Spirit *(1 Cor. 2:13)*. Paul was a minister and witness of the reality of God.

An effective minister is one who has a revelation of God and not just information. *What is revelation?* It is the supernatural knowledge and insight that the Holy Spirit imparts into our hearts. It is wise to get all of the information possible. Ignorance is one of the worst enemies. However, information about God is not enough. We need an increasing revelation of Jesus—a revelation that will produce transformation in and through us.

The School of Prophets

In Samuel's time there existed what was called *"the company of prophets"* or the *"school of prophets."* These men were very much aware of the music and knew the power that it had when directed by the Spirit. On one occasion, Samuel said to Saul:

'As you approach the town, you will meet *a procession of prophets coming down from the high place with lyres, tambourines, flutes and harps being played before them*, and they will be prophesying. *The Spirit of the Lord will come upon you in power* and you will prophesy with them... you will be changed into a different person' *(1 Sam. 10:5-6, NIV).*

When Saul met with the company of prophets, the prophetic anointing was so strongly flowing through the music that the Spirit of God came with power upon Saul, and he prophesied with them. Saul was not the same man.

Where did the prophets come from? They had just been on the mountain of God, in the glory realm, *in His Presence.* Do we know the mountain of God and what it produces in us? Does our music have the same impact as that of the prophets, or does it not affect anybody?

The Teacher that gave classes in the school of prophets continues the classes in the present. He is *the Holy Spirit of God.* Register in his school. He is the best *Teacher* around; He'll teach you all you need to know. If you honor and obey Him, I can promise you something. *You will come to know Jesus in a deeper way. And you will transmit His reality.*

- To Meditate -

✓ A prophetic worshiper is someone that communicates the reality God's presence. This reality affects the atmosphere of a place and is sensed and perceived for those who are present.

✓ Ezekiel was a communicator of the divine message. He did not speak his own words nor transmit a dead form from the past. He spoke what he heard. *He was the voice of God for his generation.*

✓ The Lord looks for Levites that are connected to Him, musicians that not only play, but also perceive the message of the heart of God.

✓ The frequency of the Spirit of God is real, and there are sounds and words found there. Prophetic worshipers discover His signal and transmit it to all men.

Chapter 4

When the Anointing Flows

As we learn to follow the Holy Spirit, our hearts will grow in the knowledge of God, and gradually, the weight of His reality over us will become more tangible. Our music will not be dead anymore, but will reflect the power and the presence of God, imparting the life of the Spirit to everyone that listens and participates in it.

Music in general, has the capacity to touch the emotions of man (the soul), but the music that comes from the presence of God can awaken and revive the most intimate part of man—his spirit.

The music of His presence flows through anointed vessels. Further on in the book we will look at what being anointed by God implies and represents, but in this chapter we will briefly look at the results of being anointed.

When the anointing of the Holy Spirit flows through prophetic worshipers diverse manifestations begin to occur. The heavens and the spiritual atmosphere of the place change; the river of God flows with power and imparts life to that which was dead; the chains break, and the prison doors open; hearts become receptive to the Word of God; the sounds of His presence penetrate the spirit, bringing a real and profound awareness of His presence.

The River of God

> "For I will pour water on him who is thirsty, and floods on
> the dry ground; I will pour My Spirit on your descendants,
> and My blessing on your offspring; They will spring up
> among the grass like willows by the watercourses"
> *(Is.44:3).*

In this portion of the Scripture one key word *is "pour
out."* The Lord promises to pour out water on the thirsty and
rivers over the dry land. In other words, He promises to pour
out His *Holy Spirit.*

When the musicians and singers are anointed, the river
of the Holy Spirit flows through the melody and the harmony,
using the music to refresh and flood His people. Each note
and each word are like fresh water in the middle of a desert.
On the other hand, when the music does not have the touch of
God, despite its beauty and careful arrangement, it feels
hollow, empty, and dead. Only the Spirit of God can impart
life.

While the prophet Ezekiel contemplated how water
came out from below the threshold of the house of God, the
man said unto him:

> "This water flows toward the eastern region, goes down
> into the valley, and enters the sea. When it reaches the sea,
> its waters are healed... every living thing that moves,
> wherever the rivers go, will live... and everything will
> live wherever the river goes" *(Ez.47:8, 9).*

The waters of life descended to the desert and entered
the *Dead Sea*, making it live, fresh and pure. They were waters
that came from the very presence of God, being full of Him.

When the *Holy Spirit* moves in our worship, He does not just change the desert into a spring; He also gives life to everything that is dead *(Job 33:4)*. Many times the congregation that is before us seems like the *Dead Sea*, completely lifeless. The only way to change this is to go deep into the river of God. Then, our music will be an arm, and extension of this river, and everything that enters into His River will live.

In reference to this point, some time ago I heard the testimony of a sister in the Lord who had a dream. In this dream she found herself in a large Christian gathering, and she could see a worship leader leading the people to God's presence. Meanwhile, a man was brought on a stretcher to the altar (up front), and to her surprise, the man was dead. Without being distracted by this, the worship leader spontaneously began to play and sing out a new song. When the woman heard this, she began to cry because she could feel the presence of God in the music. While this glorious harmony filled the place, she marveled at how *the dead man came to life*. The man opened his eyes, got up, took his stretcher, and joined the congregation, which had never ceased praising God.

Upon awakening, the woman began to pray. She asked the Lord to reveal the meaning of the dream. The Holy Spirit revealed to her that this happens when the power of His presence flows through prophetic worshipers. The spiritually and naturally dead people are resurrected, the sick are healed, the oppressed are freed, and the wounded are cured.

The best book I have found on the subject of the River of God is *"Following the River"* by Bob Sorge. I would highly encourage the reader to get it — what the Lord has shown Bob will transform you and take you deeper into the River of God's presence.

The Chains Break and the Prison Doors Open

When the power of God flows in music, faith and liberty are imparted to the people.

> But at midnight Paul and Silas were praying and singing hymns to God, and the prisoners were listening... Suddenly there was a great earthquake...the foundations of the prison were shaken; and immediately all the doors were opened and everyone's chains were loosed (*Acts 16:25, 26*).

Paul and Silas prayed, singing hymns to God. The music that came from their mouths was full of supernatural power, the *power of the Holy Spirit*. They found themselves in a very unpleasant situation in which they could have easily complained. Perhaps they could have directed their songs to resist the opposition, but they didn't do it that way. Paul and Silas lifted up their voices in praise to God, focusing solely on Him. Then, the power of the Holy Spirit that was active in their praise shook the foundations of the prison, opened the doors, and freed all the prisoners from their chains.

This is what happens when prophetic worshipers minister. They are conduits of the power of God. No prison or chain of darkness can resist because the glorious freedom of the Spirit is in action.

> Now, the Lord is the Spirit: and wherever the Spirit of the Lord is, *he gives freedom (2 Cor. 3:17, NLT)*.

Let us allow the Holy Spirit to move through us. Let us not limit or stop Him. Dare to lose control and give it completely to Him. *Experience His freedom.*

The Ground is Prepared

Through anointed worship the hearts of the people become softer and are prepared to receive the seed of God's word. If the seed falls over hard and dry ground it cannot penetrate, and so it stays on the surface without producing any fruit. The ground should be plowed and prepared to receive the seed. It is the river of God that softens the soil, and when that river flows in music, it prepares hearts to receive God's revelation.

> *While the harpist was playing,* the hand of the Lord came upon Elisha... (*2 Kings 3:15-16, NIV*).

This is a very graphic example. The music of the harpist prepared the atmosphere so that Elisha had the revelation of the Word of God. This anointed melody elevated him to the spiritual realm where he could hear the voice of God very clearly.

There is no ground or heart so hard that it can resist the power of God's presence. We need to be sensitive to the Holy Spirit and allow Him to prepare the land through worship.

The Reality of His Presence

When the touch of God is upon the worship team, the presence of Jesus becomes very real. Each musical note reflects the beauty of His lovely person.

> "I will no longer hide my face from them, for I will pour out my Spirit on the house of Israel, declares the Sovereign Lord" (Ez. 39:29, NIV).

As the Holy Spirit is poured out upon us, the face of God is then no longer something hidden and unknown. His face speaks of who He is. *It speaks of His Presence revealed*. Many know the works of God, but His face is unknown to them. It is difficult for me to recognize someone by just looking at his hands. It is necessary for me to hear his **voice** and see his **face** to know who it is. *To know God's face is to truly know Him.*

In the measure in which the Holy Spirit is poured out upon us, the revelation of God's nature and personality becomes greater, to such an extent that we will become speechless. If seeing what He does amazes us, imagine when we behold who He is.

Think about this—the apostle John was with Jesus, the worker of miracles, for three years. He was overwhelmed by His power and the wisdom of His words. Nevertheless, one day on the island of Patmos, being in the Spirit, he had a deeper revelation of Jesus. His shock and amazement was so great that he fell, as if dead, at His feet.

We can be standing, watching the miracles that He does and how a measure of His power is manifested, but *will we be able to remain standing before the glory of His presence?* I don't think so; however, I also believe that as was with John, the Lord is going to strengthen us so we may stand and minister to the people.

There is nothing more beautiful than the manifest Presence of God. Those who have experienced it do not settle for anything less.

His manifest Presence in our worship makes the difference. No program or religious form satisfies the profound thirst of man, *only the Presence of Christ*. The music of His Presence is like the brightness of the face of Christ upon *His* Church.

The Glory of God

> ...indeed it came to pass, when the trumpeters and singers were as one, to make one sound to be heard in praising and thanking the Lord, and when they lifted up their voice with the trumpets and cymbals and instruments of music, and praised the Lord, saying: *"For He is good, For His mercy endures forever,"* that the house, the house of the Lord, was filled with a cloud, so that the priests could not continue ministering because of the cloud; for the glory of the Lord filled the house of God *(2 Chr. 5:13-14).*

In the measure that the singers lifted up their voices and worshiped the Lord, the glory of the God of Israel descended and filled the temple.

Isn't that what we desire in our meetings? I believe that every prophetic worshiper seeks and desires for this to happen. Even more than it being our desire, it is something that God is restoring today. Not just inside of four walls, but everywhere the temple of God *(His Church)* resides.

The days when we will experience the *"crushing weight"* of the glory of God are soon arriving. A movement of heavenly glory will soon sweep the nations. The knowledge of the beauty and the splendor of our Lord will fill the earth. That is why today, the Lord is seeking hearts that are surrendered to His Spirit and ready to obey His Word — a generation that will prepare the way for the revelation of His glory.

- To Meditate -

✓ When the musicians and singers are anointed, the river of the Holy Spirit flows through the melody and the harmony, using the music to refresh and flood His people.

✓ When the power of God flows in music, faith and liberty are imparted to the people.

✓ It is the river of God that softens the soil, and when that river flows in music, it prepares hearts to receive His Word.

✓ His Presence in our worship makes the difference.

✓ The days when we will experience the *"crushing weight"* of the glory of God are soon arriving. A movement of heavenly glory will soon sweep the nations. The knowledge of the beauty and the splendor of our Lord will fill the earth. That is why today, the Lord is seeking hearts that are surrendered to His Spirit and ready to obey His Word—a generation that will prepare the way for the revelation of His glory

Chapter 5

The Sweet Psalmist of Israel

In the previous four chapters, we have briefly described the glorious difference that the anointing of God brings to our worship and ministry. Now, we will dedicate some chapters to study how the same anointing is powerful to bring change to our souls.

There is a work of holiness that the Spirit of Truth jealously desires to do in our hearts. The Holy Spirit will not rest until the nature of God becomes ours. Be sure of this— He absolutely loves His job and is dedicated and tenacious about it. Oh Yes! Our Divine Helper will not stop until we look, feel, think, speak and act like Jesus.

Let's start our journey into this subject by observing the life of a young man from Bethlehem.

> Thus says David the son of Jesse; thus says the man raised up on high, the anointed of the God of Jacob, and the sweet psalmist of Israel: "The Spirit of the Lord spoke by me, and His word was on my tongue *(2 Sam. 23:1-2)*.

The author of second Samuel couldn't have used more beautiful and expressive words. These two verses are full of life and faithfully describe part of the history of David. Being the youngest in his family, he was raised up to a place that, perhaps, he had never imagined at his young age. They called him the *"Sweet Psalmist of Israel"*, and we continue singing many of his songs today. They also identified him as *"The anointed of the God of Jacob"*, and because of this he became who he was. The Spirit of the Lord put sweetness in his song—took him from among the sheep and raised him up— fought his battles and made him a conqueror.

All this began one day in Bethlehem. The prophet Samuel found himself in the house of Jesse; his mission was to anoint the next king of Israel. Jesse brought his eldest son, Eliab, before the prophet, and then his six other sons, but the Lord did not choose any of them. *God had placed His eyes upon the one who was after His own heart.*

> Then Samuel asked, "Are these all the sons you have?" "There is still the youngest," Jesse replied.... So Jesse sent for him. He was ruddy and handsome, with pleasant eyes. And the Lord said, "This is the one; anoint him." So as David stood there among his brothers, *Samuel took the olive oil he had brought and poured it on David's head. And the Spirit of the Lord came mightily upon him from that day on"* (1 Sam. 16:11-13, NLT).

When David was anointed, everything changed. He didn't find himself alone anymore, there was a wonderful person that surrounded him— *the Holy Spirit*. He took his harp and played the same as always, but the surrounding atmosphere was distinct, there was somebody else there. He could perceive the presence of a person that he had not known before but one he would come to know very well.

Seven Qualities of David

King David certainly possessed many faults and made several serious mistakes, but in this chapter we are going to focus on seven of his virtues.

Now the Spirit of the Lord had departed from Saul, and an evil spirit from the Lord tormented him. Saul's attendants said to him.... "Search for someone who can play the harp. *He will play when the evil sprit from God comes upon you and you will feel better."* So Saul said.... "Find someone who plays well and bring him to me" (*1 Sam. 16:14-17, NIV*).

In the times when David was still a teenager, Saul was King of Israel. But because of Saul's disobedience and rebellion, the Holy Spirit departed from him. As a result, God allowed an evil spirit to torment him. The servants of Saul realized the problem and suggested bringing in a musician that knew how to play the harp. Saul, in a state of despair agreed to this, but asked for a musician that played well. One of Saul's servants recalled seeing a youth in Bethlehem and began to describe his qualities.

1. He Knew How to Play

One of the servants answered, "I have seen a son of Jesse of Bethlehem who **knows how to play the harp**" (*1 Sam. 16:18, NIV*).

The first virtue that David had was knowing how to play the harp. In my opinion, he knew how to play in two ways— in the *natural* and the *spiritual*.

The natural is the technical knowledge. It's knowing how to do something. This knowledge is not more important than the spiritual, but it is very essential. For example, if I only know how to play in G major, the Holy Spirit will only be able to use me playing in G major (In this case, the technical knowledge is very limited). If I know how to play in four different keys, He will be able to use me in those four. If I know how to play in all keys, He will be able to use me in all of them. The same thing happens with the rhythm, if I can only execute two types of rhythms, God will only be able to use those. If I master all the rhythms, the field in which I move in will be much wider. The greater the technique, the more we will have to offer and surrender to God. *He deserves the best, and excellence is pleasing to Him.*

The spiritual area was the one most developed in David's music. It is interesting to note that there were undoubtedly many musicians in Israel who possessed excellent technical skills, but I believe that the servant of the king was referring to something else. He knew that Saul was being tormented by an evil sprit, and a musician that just played well would not help in the least. A spiritual answer was required for this spiritual need, and the answer was David. Somehow this servant knew that the Presence of God was manifested when this youth from Bethlehem played.

After being with Saul, David proved that all the servant had said was true.

> And so it was, whenever the spirit from God was upon Saul, that David would take a harp and play it with his hand. Then Saul would become refreshed and well, and the distressing spirit would depart from him *(I Sam. 16:23)*.

Do you know why the evil spirit departed? Because it could not tolerate the Presence of God that flowed in the music. David played the harp with his hand so that the heavens would open over that place and the Holy Spirit of God descended.

Let me present before you some challenging thoughts and questions. *Do we know how to play like David, or do we just play well? Is the Holy Spirit active in our music?* These days the needs and the problems of the people continue to be spiritual; they need more than just good music. They are desperate to feel and encounter God in our music.

There is only one who can give life to that which is dead: *the Holy Spirit.* David possessed something that many confuse with talent. When he played, the atmosphere of the place changed— a wind began to blow, and this wind brought *Someone* soaring on its wings.

> He parted the heavens and came down... He mounted the cherubim and flew; **he soared on the wings of the wind**... Out of *the brightness of his presence* bolts of lightning blazed forth *(2 Sam. 22:10-13 NIV).*

These are not just fancy words; it is the reality that David had seen and experienced when the Lord descended. He witnessed a God that came with power and glory, bringing liberty and defeating his enemies *(2 Sam. 22:14 -20).*

When God bows down the heavens and descends, the wind of the Spirit begins to blow, and there is *One* that soars upon His wings—the King of Kings and Lord of Lords. He rides on the wings of the wind *(Ps. 104:3).* At the shining of His glory that comes through the music, lives, which are like coal, are lit once again, and hearts begin to burn in His presence.

Now, please notice that David did not achieve this musical gift on one day; it was a process. He became the sweet singer of Israel because the Holy Spirit taught him to minister in an effective way. Thanks to this formidable Teacher, David learned to move in the supernatural, a dimension that the natural man cannot perceive nor understand *(I Cor. 2:14)*.

David moved in the Spirit, and the things of the Spirit of God are foolish for those who are in the flesh because they cannot perceive them. The language of the flesh comes from logic and reason, but the language of the Spirit comes from faith. Because of this, when David wanted to face Goliath, some criticized him and told him that he was not able to do it *(I Sam. 17: 28, 33)*. It was logical that a boy could not defeat a giant, but the anointing that was upon David had given him the capacity. Therefore, what an army was not able to do, a boy that was working in the supernatural could.

The same thing happens in worship; there can be an army of musicians, well equipped like the army of Saul, but if the *anointing* is not upon them they will not be able to obtain the victory, only defeat and failure.

Great are the victories that are not dependent on the arm of the flesh, but dependent absolutely on the Holy Spirit *(2 Chr. 32:8)*. If we want to know how to play like David, we need to go to the school of the Spirit, a school that lasts our entire lives.

2. A Brave Man

"I have seen a son of Jesse of Bethlehem who knows how to play the harp. **He is a brave man**..." *(I Sam. 16:18 NIV)*.

Added to knowing how to play, the sweet psalmist of Israel was *valiant, bold, fearless, brave*. A brave person is someone who takes risks. He who is a coward never risks anything.

But David said to Saul, "Your servant used to keep his father's sheep, and when a lion or a bear came and took a lamb out of the flock, I went out after it and struck it, and delivered the lamb from its mouth; and when it arose against me, I caught it by its beard, and struck and killed it. Your servant has killed both lion and bear; and this uncircumcised Philistine will be like one of them...(*1 Sam. 17: 34-36*).

David could have played the fool when the bear and the lion came, nobody was going to realize that one lamb was missing. Besides, they weren't even his sheep; he could have easily taken an attitude of *safety first*. Nevertheless, David risked his life every time. He did not fear Goliath because for him Goliath was like the bear; and the God that had saved David from the bear would also save him from the giant.

How is it that David could advance towards something that all others fled from? There was one determining factor in David that drove him forward: *the faith of God imparted to his heart,* a fruit of his relationship with the Holy Spirit *(Gal. 5:22).*

... who through faith subdued kingdoms, worked righteousness, obtained promises, stopped the mouths of lions, quenched the violence of fire, escaped the edge of the sword, out of weakness were made strong, became valiant in battle, turned to flight the armies of the aliens (*Heb.11: 33-34*).

In the Bible, the people that made the difference in the long run were those who were filled with faith. It was not an intellectual faith that came from a mental ascent; rather a real faith that came from the heart and that is the result of gazing at the Author and Finisher of our faith—Jesus. This is an increasing faith that believes the impossible, speaks the things that aren't as if they were, and helps to keep us advancing.

Now, in leading worship, we need to be brave to give up control of the service and give God room. Many times we like to be safe rather than risk anything. We prefer to have control and cling to our program because outside of this we do not know what to do. Perhaps, the Holy Spirit prompts us to go in one direction and we don't follow Him because the unknown scares us—that which we have not programmed.

Now, don't get me wrong. There is nothing bad about planning or having a structure. In fact, it is necessary. *But*, we cannot allow our programs to control us. If we do, in the end we will find ourselves bound up, prisoners, not able to follow what the Holy Spirit dictates.

It is time to surrender and give ourselves completely to the Lord, allowing Him to carry us in the direction that He wants to go, learning to follow Him even though we can't see the path ahead.

3. Strong and Vigorous

"The son of Jesse is a talented harp player. Not only that; he is brave **and strong....**" (*1 Sam. 16:18, NLT*).

The other quality that Saul's servant noted in David was his strength and vigor. A vigorous person is full of power and energy.

Who gave David this vigor? "God is my strength and power, and He makes my way perfect. He makes my feet like the feet of deer, and sets me on my high places. He teaches my hands to make war, so that my arms can bend a bow of bronze" (*2 Sam. 22: 33-35*).

David recognized the source of his strength; he did not try to bring glory to himself but always gave the glory to God. In other words, he said, *"I cannot do anything without Him; I am completely helpless if He does not give me strength."*

Strength and vigor are not natural to a musician. We tend to be nostalgic and melancholy. This characteristic has the potential to open a door for *depression,* which is a deadly enemy. *Depression* is not usually a sickness, but an unclean spirit that consumes and destroys those afflicted. It robs them of their strength, vigor, energy, and faith. They can sink into such an extreme despair that it makes them vulnerable to any attack from the devil. *Depression* normally takes advantage of difficult circumstances and times of crisis. However, sometimes it has complete dominion over a life.

If you find yourself in this state, *do not fear;* the devil comes to kill, steal, and destroy, but Jesus Christ wants to give you abundant life *(Jn. 10:10).* All you have to do is look to the Lord, seek Him and depend on Him as the strength of your life.

Happy are *those who are strong in the Lord...* When they walk through the Valley of Weeping, it will become a place of refreshing springs, where pools of blessing collect after the rains! *They will continue to grow stronger (Ps. 84:5–7 NLT).*

4. A Warrior

"I have seen a son of Jesse of Bethlehem ... He is a brave man and **a warrior**" *(I Sam. 16:18, NIV).*

The son of Jesse knew how to fight, and he didn't do it with his might, but in the power of the Spirit. *"The Philistine commanders continued to go out to battle, and as often as they did, David met with more success than the rest of Saul's officers, and his name became well known" (I Sam. 18:30, NIV).*

The servants of Saul were also men of war, but David was more successful than all of them. When David went out to war, he did great damage to the enemy forces. The Philistine armies fled before him. The servants of Saul were part of the people of God, and they went fully armed to the battle but did not play a big part in helping to win the wars. In fact, these soldiers did so little that this one young boy had more success than all of them.

Saul's army represents those that fight in the flesh. Men of war that trust more in their skills and abilities than in the Holy Spirit. As a result, they lack His power.

Saul's army demonstrated that they lacked the *"real thing"* by taking the following attitude:

"When Saul and all Israel heard these words of the Philistine, they were dismayed and greatly afraid" (1 Sam. 17:11. See 17: 24).

David's actions were the exact opposite. He moved in a higher dimension, realizing that the kingdom of darkness was real. The devil does not respect the flesh, only the anointing of the Spirit. The anointed warrior does not fight in his own strength, rather in the strength of God. He does not fight in the flesh because he has learned to submit to the Holy Spirit and to move in His power. He has become an instrument His hands and follows His initiative, not his own. For this reason, the anointed soldier has, undoubtedly, more success than those who fight in the flesh.

Those that fight in the flesh make a lot of noise, but lack results. Because their whole battle is born in the flesh and not in the Spirit. *"That which is born of the flesh is flesh, and that which is born of the Spirit is spirit." (Jn 3:6).* Only what is born of the Spirit works in the kingdom of God.

The apostle Paul declares that the weapons of God are not carnal but *"mighty through God" (2 Cor.10:3-4)*. It is because our weapons are found in God that they are powerful and effective to destroy the strongholds. If our weapons are not God-given, even our best efforts, tenacity, and good intentions that motivate us will be useless against the enemy.

The outward appearance of the soldier isn't what counts either *(When David killed Goliath, he didn't look anything like a soldier)*. What really counts is the Spirit that works and moves in and with us.

> For they did not gain possession of the land by their own sword, nor did their own arm save them; but it was Your right hand, Your arm, and the light of Your countenance *(Ps. 44: 3)*.

It is not because of our sword or our might that we conquer the land. It is because of the power of His Presence.

Another problem of those who fight in the flesh is that they fight as if they have to win the battle. On the other hand, those that fight in the Spirit fight in a battle that has already been won. *"Having disarmed principalities and powers, He made a public spectacle of them, triumphing over them in it" (Col. 2:15).* *"So when Jesus had received the sour wine, He said, 'It is finished!' And bowing His head, He gave up His spirit" (Jn. 19:30).* Jesus Christ gave us the victory. The defeat of the devil is an act finished on the cross; it is a legal contract to which nothing can be added or taken away. It is finished! We should walk in the triumph of the cross announcing that which has already been done. Every human effort that pretends to exalt and crown itself above Calvary is blasphemy against God and the blood of His Son.

Let the high praises of God be in their mouth, and a two-
edged sword in their hand, to execute vengeance on the
nations, and punishments on the peoples; to bind their
kings with chains, and their nobles with fetters of iron; to
execute on them the written judgment—This honor have
all His saints. Praise the Lord! *(Ps. 149:6-9).*

The warriors that move in the anointing exalt the Lord
with their voices and execute vengeance and punishment
upon the enemy with the sword of the Spirit, which is the
Word of God *(Eph. 6:17);* these men bind the kings with chains
and fetters of iron; they execute justice that was already
decreed on the cross. They celebrate and declare on high the
victory of a resurrected Christ, seated at the right hand of the
Father, far above every principality and power, might and
dominion, above every name that is named and with all things
under His feet.

5. Prudent in Speech

"I have seen a son of Jesse… who plays skillfully, a valiant,
a man of war, **prudent in speech**" *(1 Sam. 16:18 Amp).*

Another one of David's qualities was the prudence in
his words. *Prudence is a virtue that prevents and evades mistakes
and danger.* David was prudent in his words because he
refrained his tongue. *"When words are many, sin is not absent,
but he who holds his tongue is wise"* (Pr. 10:19, NIV).
Now, I am not going to comment much more about
David on this point. But once again, please allow me to present
some challenging scenarios.
Perhaps you are an efficient warrior that flows in the
anointing of the Spirit, and the last point is not a novelty for

you. But let us expose ourselves together to the light of God's presence in order to carefully examine the possibility of finding no prudence in our words and comments. Shall we? All right, let's start with the tongue. From time to time we are very far from being wise, participating in *gossip, criticism, murmuring, slander, etc.*

Let's pay attention to words from James:

> And *the tongue* is a flame of fire. It is full of wickedness that can ruin your whole life. It can turn the entire course of your life into a blazing flame of destruction, for it is set on fire by hell itself... *Sometimes it praises our Lord and Father and sometimes it breaks out into curses against those who have been made in the image of God.* And so blessing and cursing come pouring out of the same mouth. Surely, my brothers and sisters, *this is not right!* Jam. 3:6:9-10 NLT.

The irresponsible tongue possesses a destructive potential. It can bless God, but also curse men. The imprudent live seated on the throne of the *judge*, and do not measure the damage of their judgments and comments. Criticizing the mistakes of others is the biggest normal pastime for this person; his nature feeds upon gossip and complaint.

From the very beginning God condemned this:

> *Do not spread slanderous gossip among your people.* Do not try to get ahead at the cost of your neighbor's life (*Lev. 19: 16, KJV*).

Gossip is similar to a powerful computer virus that enters the system and contaminates it to the point of destruction. Likewise, gossip enters into a group of people and does not stop until this group has been divided and eventually ruined.

Participating in gossip is comparable to attempting to take the life of your neighbor. It is being used as an instrument for the devil. God knew of this danger and, therefore, commanded the entire nation of Israel to not gossip. Nevertheless, the people of God did not obey, and the prophet Isaiah came, declaring: *"For Jerusalem stumbled, and Judah is fallen, because their tongue and their doings Are against the Lord, to provoke the eyes of His glory"* (Is. 3:8). Let us take care... so that we do not find ourselves provoking His presence with our tongues.

Brothers, do not slander one another... who are you to judge your neighbor? *(James 4:11-12, NIV).*

The Word of God commands us to not speak badly of one another. Are we fulfilling this commandment?

It is sad to see how some prophetic worshipers beat their partners with their words. They use their tongues to wound and hurt their fellow servants without counting the cost. This gives place to gossip and strife, jealousy and envy — speaking and defending themselves *as if they were in a competition*. They despise what God has given to others and compare themselves, hoping to prove themselves superior.

Jesus harshly condemned this attitude *(Mt. 24: 51)*, as did the apostle Paul:

"Do nothing out of selfish ambition or vain conceit, but *in humility consider others better than yourselves*. Each of you should look not only to your own interests, but also to the interests of others" *(Phil 2:3-4, NIV).*

Motivation is very important. Knowing the reason for doing what I am doing is fundamental. If I achieve things through selfish ambition, then bitter jealousy, strife, fighting, wars, murmuring, and the like are always the result *(James 3:13-4:12). But*, if I learn to walk according to the *"Golden Key"* that the apostle gives in Philippians, there will be no room in my life for these sorts of things.

The Golden Key is*:*

> ➤ *To consider, esteem, and treat others better than myself.* This way, I will never feel superior, and as a result, I will not beat my fellow servants.

Are we being prudent in our speech? Does our tongue bless God and curse our brothers at the same time? Have we learned to refrain our lips? It is necessary that we ask ourselves these questions so that we may align with the Word of God.

Quite honestly, many people just take these things with a "grain of salt", not giving them any importance. They do not realize the damage that an *evil tongue* can have. The lack of confidentiality and discretion constantly feeds the mistrust that exists among brethren. It is much more tempting to make public the faults and intimate secrets of your neighbor than to intercede before the Lord for him. We should return to prudence, repent, and walk in integrity.

Who may worship in your sanctuary, Lord? Who may enter your presence on your holy hill? Those who lead blameless lives and do what is right, speaking the truth from sincere hearts. *Those who refuse to slander others or harm their neighbors or speak evil of their friends"* (Ps.15:1–3, NLT).

David realized and understood that he could not abide in the presence of God if he was not careful in this area.

6. An Attractive Person

"I have seen a son of Jesse… who plays skillfully, a valiant,
a man of war, prudent in speech… **an attractive
person**" *(1 Sam. 16:18 Amp).*

David's sixth quality was his *attractiveness—his beauty.*
This does not only speak of his outer appearance, but also an
inner reality.

There are people that are really good looking in their
physical appearance, but when you get to know their
personality you might conclude that they are nasty and
unpleasant, full of poison and evil.

The inner beauty is what counts with God. His eyes do
not look upon outward appearances, but rather upon the
heart. A person with a beautiful heart is someone full of
freshness and life. Such a person inspires and transmits the
love of God to those around him.

David's beauty was not his own; it stemmed from God
whom he loved.

One thing I ask of the Lord, this is what I seek: that I may
dwell in the house of the Lord all the days of my life, *to
gaze upon the beauty of the Lord and to seek him* in
his temple *(Ps. 27:4, NIV).*

That which David sought passionately, and totally
consumed him, was a desire to be in the Presence of the Lord,
to behold His beauty. The result was that this beauty stayed
with him and began to become part of him, making him
attractive, different, and beautiful.

The beauty of God is powerfully reflected in music.
When His Presence comes, His beauty and majesty is reflected
in the harmony and the melody of an instrument or a voice.

It's like a fresh revelation of Jesus, which is the most beautiful and stunning person in the universe.

> In that day the Branch of the Lord shall be **beautiful and glorious**; and the fruit of the earth shall be excellent and appealing for those of Israel who have escaped (*Is. 4:2*)

The Branch of the Lord is a messianic title for Jesus, the only begotten of the Father, the manifestation of His glory and beauty.

We are swiftly approaching the day when the Lord will unveil His beauty to the nations. The stadiums and open fields around the world will be filled with multitudes of lovesick worshipers—millions of human beings singing songs of love to the One that has captivated their hearts—the Man Christ Jesus.

One of the main ways in which the Branch of the Lord will branch out is through a global worship movement. The music and songs from heaven will sweep across the earth. *Make no mistake about it*—He is raising up a multicultural generation of prophetic worshipers. They will shine with the glory of God and portray the beauty of the Lord to the nations.

7. The Lord's Presence

> "I have seen a son of Jesse… who plays skillfully, a valiant, a man of war, prudent in speech… an attractive person, and **The Lord is with him**" (*1 Sam. 16:18, Amp*).

All the prior qualities are simply impossible if God is not with us. He is our life and our strength; without His presence we cannot do anything.

The prophet Jeremiah declared: *"But the Lord is with me as a mighty, awesome One."* (*Jer. 20:11*). David, as well as many other men of the Bible, experienced the presence of God with them. Moses was promised the following: *'My presence shall go with thee, and I shall give thee rest'* Joshua also heard these words: *'...As I was with Moses, I shall also be with you; I shall never leave you, nor forsake you'*. Throughout the entire Old Testament we see that God was with His servants, but He also spoke of the day that He would be in them:

"I will put My Spirit within you and cause you to walk in My statutes, and you will keep My judgments and do them" (*Ez. 36:27*).

This indicated the New Covenant. Through the redemptive work of Christ on the cross, God would not only be *"with"* us, but *"in"* us, as well. Jesus referred to this: *'At that day you will know that I am in My Father, and you in Me, and I in you""* (*Jn. 14: 20*).

In other words, they would know the reality of His Presence inside of them — *not just around them*. This is something that David and all the other men of God in the Old Testament did not experience. They only experienced God with and upon them, but not in them. We live under the New Covenant, where the Presence of God dwells in the hearts of His people. This is the reality of the new creation, *His Presence living inside of us*.

Walking in Wisdom

Let's open our hearts to God in truth, allowing His Spirit to work and mold our lives. The same One who imparted these qualities to the sweet psalmist of Israel wants to give them to you. *Believe it!* And get to know the Holy Spirit because these virtues are the fruit that He produces.

- To Meditate -

✓ Do we know how to play like David, or do we just play well? These days the needs and the problems of the people continue to be spiritual; they need more than just good music.

✓ Participating in gossip is comparable to attempting to take the life of your neighbor. It is being used as an instrument for the devil. We must return to prudence, repent, and walk in integrity.

✓ The anointed warrior does not fight in his own strength, rather in the strength of God. He does not fight in the flesh because he has learned to submit to the Holy Spirit and to move in His power.

✓ When the music of His Presence flows, the beauty and majesty of God is reflected in the harmony and the melody of an instrument or a voice. It's like a fresh revelation of the Man Christ Jesus, which is the most beautiful and stunning person in the universe.

✓ One of the main ways in which the Branch of the Lord will branch out is through a global worship movement. The music and songs from heaven will sweep across the earth. *Make no mistake about it* — He is raising up a multicultural generation of prophetic worshipers. They will shine with the glory of God and portray the beauty of the Lord to the nations.

Chapter 6

A Broken Vessel

To understand the subject of this chapter is key for every prophetic worshiper as it is for every person in the Kingdom of God. In the journey of our lives, there are seasons of suffering and brokenness. Difficult times in where we find ourselves facing rejection, disappointment, betrayal, tragedies, pain and all kinds of trouble. Some of these things are caused by our lack of wisdom and sin. But most times, in the economy and genius of God for His children, He orchestrates and allows hardship and adversity to come our way.

David, a Broken Vessel

In one of his songs, David proclaims: *"...I am like a broken vessel"* *(Ps. 31: 12).* Why his soul was wounded to such an extent that he compared it to a broken vessel?

Have mercy on me, O Lord, for I am in trouble; my eye wastes away with grief, Yes, my soul and my body! ....I am a reproach among all my enemies, but especially among my neighbors, and am repulsive to my acquaintances; those who see me outside flee from me. I am forgotten like a

dead man, out of mind; *I am like a broken vessel*. For I hear
the slander of many; Fear is on every side; while they take
counsel together against me, they scheme to take away
my life *(Ps. 31: 9 –13)*.

David was in danger of death; the slanderous words
spoken against him did not cease, and fear assaulted him on
all sides; anguish, pain, and sadness were transformed into
his daily bread. All this left him spent to the point of leaving
him weak and needy.

*Why did God allow David, His anointed, to pass through all
this?* The plan of God was to break him; perhaps, David did
not understand at that moment, but the Lord had a purpose
with all this. If his vessel had not been broken, he never would
have had the revelation and the knowledge of God that he
had. Affliction and difficulty obligated David to seek the Lord
until finding Him. Besides, it was from this broken vessel
that sprung forth anointed songs that are eternal.

Joseph, a Fruitful Tree

Another man in the Scriptures that experienced an
intense breaking process was Joseph. One day he looked at
his second son, who had just been born, and when giving
him his name declared:

And the name of the second he called Ephraim: "For God
has caused me to be fruitful in the land of my affliction."
(Gen. 41:52).

His words reveal one of the purposes of affliction in our
lives— *to produce fruit*. Everyone who has studied the story
of Joseph knows what he had to pass through. Just like David,
Joseph had promises on his life, but until these were fulfilled,

he traversed through a dark valley. *"He sent a man before them, even Joseph, who was sold for a servant: whose feet they hurt with fetters: he was laid in iron: until the time that this word came: the word of the Lord tried him"* (Ps. 105:17–19). Could it be true, all that the Lord had showed him in those dreams when he was an adolescent? Certainly they were true, but it took time for them to become reality.

Years later, Jacob, Joseph's father, blessed him saying:

> "Joseph is a fruitful tree, a fruitful tree beside a fountain. His branches reach over the wall. He has been attacked by archers, who shot at him and harassed him. But his bow remained strong, and his arms were strengthened by the Mighty One of Jacob" (*Gen. 49:22–24, NLT*).

They sorely grieved him and hated him, and he was wounded by the arrows that came at him from the *"archers"* (*a phrase that Jacob used in reference to Joseph's brothers*). He was a victim of lies, envy, and deceit. He suffered hate, and through the years withstood being forgotten.

Nevertheless, God permitted it all. God saw the finished work, *"a fruitful tree."* His life was exemplary. Like David, he was broken with the purpose of bringing forth fruit. Not only did he become a blessing for two nations, the world was affected by his ministry (*Gen. 41: 57*).

Joseph is a type of Christ. The affliction and the breaking that he suffered (*if you could at all compare it*) are similar to what our Lord suffered.

Jesus, the Lamb that was Slain

"He is despised and rejected by men, a Man of sorrows and acquainted with grief. And we hid, as it were, our faces from Him; He was despised, and we did not esteem Him" (*Is. 53:3*).

If anyone has experienced that which is described above, it was Jesus- *the Son of God*. There is no one who can describe it like He; His vessel broke to the point of death, and His fruit is limitless. He poured out His soul unto death.

The fifty-third chapter of Isaiah is one of the most extraordinary chapters in the Bible; its depth is unfathomable, abounding in riches and revelation. The Father's plan was imaged here: *"But it was the Lord's good plan to crush him and fill him with grief..." Is. 53: 10 (NLT)*. The will of the Father was to crush His Son, and He did it in this way: *"...filling him with grief..."* But it did not end there:

'Yet it pleased the Lord to bruise Him; He has put Him to grief. When You make His soul an offering for sin, He shall see His seed, He shall prolong His days, and the pleasure of the Lord shall prosper in His hand. He shall see the labor of His soul, and be satisfied. By His knowledge My righteous Servant shall justify many, for He shall bear their iniquities' (Is 53:10-11).

The Son would see the fruit of affliction of His soul and would be satisfied. In a form similar to that of Joseph and David, God broke His own Son with a purpose in mind — *the fruit*.

"*Behold, He struck the rock, so that the waters gushed out, and the streams overflowed*" (Ps.78:20). Jesus Christ is the rock that was smitten *(1 Cor 10:4)*. Today, we rejoice to be able to drink from His waters, but let's not forget that the price paid for this was very high — a price of suffering, great pain, and death.

If God was willing to break His Only Begotten Son, and even had pleasure in doing it *(because He understood the great reward — the glorious outcome of affliction)*, He will do the same with us. If the rock is not smitten, water will not spring forth; if the vessel is not broken, its treasure will not flow.

There are some circumstances that we have lived through that we do not understand completely. Maybe there are things from childhood that marked our lives and we have always asked ourselves *"Why?"* We can know this for sure — God has a purpose in everything that He does. The affliction that He allows in our lives brings with it a revelation of His love and faithfulness. *"I know, O Lord, that Your judgments are right, And that in faithfulness You have afflicted me" (Ps. 119:75).*

We should learn to see His faithfulness even when the situation is negative and painful for us. Let us trust that God's leadership over our lives — He is working for our good.

In His Hands

The feeding of the five thousand is a marvelous story in which we find the wonderful principles of brokenness.

> Then Jesus lifted up His eyes, and seeing a great multitude coming toward Him, He said to Philip, "Where shall we buy bread, that these may eat?" One of His disciples, Andrew, Simon Peter's brother, said to Him, "There is a lad here who has five barley loaves and two small fish, but what are they among so many?" *(Jn. 6: 5, 8-9).*

The loaves and fishes represent our lives. Andrew said: *"What are they among so many?"* Logically, it was not enough for the multitude, but the point was not the loaves and the fishes, but rather what the Master could do with them. **It is not what you can do; it is what Jesus can do with you when you surrender to Him.** God takes that which appears to you as nothing, He blesses it, breaks it, and multiplies it for a blessing to thousands.

> And when He had taken the five loaves and the two fish, He looked up to heaven, blessed and broke the loaves, and gave them to His disciples to set before them; and the two fish He divided among them all (*Mk. 6:41*).

First, Jesus **took** the five loaves and the two fishes; He chooses to take that which is given to Him. If we want Him to take our lives to do with them what He pleases, then we should put them in His hands, not just in word, but also in action. Then it says that Jesus **blessed** the loaves. Allow me to use play on words. *Without His blessing, it is impossible to be a blessing.* And if this blessing is real, there will also be brokenness. After this, **Jesus broke the loaves.** This is not only a type of Christ on the cross (*His body being bruised and broken for us, and then distributed for a blessing to billions of people*), but it also represents the type of breaking that God wants to work in our lives. Then, He commanded that the loaves be **distributed.** That which God does not break He does not distribute. If we allow Him to take our nothing and break it, we will be a blessing to many.

Today, Jesus continues saying, *'Bring them here to Me'* (*Matt. 14:18*). He knows that the loaves and fishes alone cannot do anything; they need to be in His hands. It is there where our lives produce fruit.

Joseph and David trusted in God enough to place their lives in His hands. Will we put our lives in His hands? We have to understand one thing — *only that which God takes, breaks, and distributes will be of blessing.*

Breaking the Vessel During Worship

There is a breaking that takes place during services, when a prophetic worshiper is leading the people into God's presence. To have the vessel break during a service is to die to one's own wisdom and knowledge. It is to surrender self to the Spirit of God so that His life flows.

We see this illustrated in the book of Judges. When *Gideon* was ready to face the enemy, he gave his men some very interesting weapons:

> Then he divided the three hundred men into three companies, and he put a trumpet into every man's hand, with empty pitchers, and torches inside the pitchers (*Jgs. 7:16*).

Trumpets, pitchers, and lamps. The trumpet represents the Word of God expressed through prophetic worship. The pitcher is like our lives. And the lamp represents the demonstration and the manifestation of the Holy Spirit. These three elements work together.

> Then the three companies blew the trumpets and broke the pitchers they held the torches in their left hands and the trumpets in their right hands for blowing—and they cried, "The sword of the Lord and of Gideon! (*Jgs. 7:20*).

Let me share with you what I see in this passage — The torch, or lamp, was found inside of the pitcher and couldn't be seen until the pitcher was broken. The lamp reflected light and could be seen from the distance. This is the symbol of the manifestation and the demonstration of the Spirit of God. It was the burning lamp in the other hand that made the trumpet sound so powerful. The pitcher, or vessel, guarded a precious treasure, and this treasure could only be seen once the pitcher was broken.

To break the vessel in a service is to stop showing ourselves so that the Holy Spirit can be shown.

As the apostle Paul said:

"And my speech and my preaching were not with persuasive words of human wisdom, but in demonstration of the Spirit and of power" (1 Cor. 2:4).

The sound of the trumpet went with the demonstration of the Spirit. **This is what determines and distinguishes this generation of prophetic worshipers — not just the sound, but the manifestation of God through the sound.**

Gideon and his men played the trumpet and broke their pitchers *(Jgs. 7:19)*. What would have happened if they had only played the trumpets and hadn't broken the pitchers? Perhaps the same thing happens with the music that comes from a life that is not broken. *The sound is persuasive and full of human wisdom but void of a demonstration of the Spirit.*

The powerful manifestation of His presence is reflected through the music when our pitcher is broken... when we step to one side and forget about ourselves.

To break the vessel is to surrender, to submit, and to die. *"Most assuredly, I say to you, unless a grain of wheat falls into the ground and dies, it remains alone; but if it dies, it produces much grain" (Jn. 12:24)*. When the corn falls to the ground, it dies; death always begins with brokenness, and everything on the outside is destroyed, completely losing its original form in order to give way to the life that is inside. Let us not remain just in the outside form, but let us die and discover the life inside, *the life of the Spirit,* which bears much fruit.

There is a Scripture that illustrates this chapter very well:

"And being in Bethany at the house of Simon the leper, as He sat at the table, a woman came having an alabaster flask of very costly oil of spikenard. Then she broke the flask and poured it on His head" *(Mk. 14:3).*

This woman broke the vessel and freed the treasure that it contained. *The beauty of the treasure did not lie in the vessel, rather in its contents.* When it was broken, the richness inside was poured out. This has a tremendous spiritual significance because true worship flows when the vessel breaks.

In our day, the Lord is raising worshipers that have been broken. They will play and sing, and as they minister, a fragrant oil of worship will be released among the nations.

- To Meditate -

✓ Without His blessing, it is impossible to be a blessing.

✓ That which God does not break He does not distribute.

✓ We have to understand one thing — *only that which God takes, breaks, and distributes will be of blessing*.

✓ To break the vessel in a service is to stop showing ourselves so that the Holy Spirit can be shown.

✓ This is what determines and distinguishes this *generation of prophetic worshipers* — not just the sound, but the manifestation of God through the sound.

✓ In our day, the Lord is raising worshipers that have been broken. They will play and sing, and as they minister, a fragrant oil of worship will be released among the nations.

Chapter 7

Holiness and Humility

Every prophetic worshiper needs to understand the importance of walking in holiness and humility. Impurity and pride are deadly enemies that have the potential of eventually killing the move of the Spirit in and through our lives.

A voice of one calling: "In the desert *prepare the way for the Lord;* make straight in the wilderness a highway for our God. Every valley shall be raised up, every mountain and hill made low.... and the glory of the Lord will be revealed, and all mankind together will see it" (*Is. 40:3-5, NIV*).

The voice of *"one"* who cried through Isaiah and John the Baptist continues today. It is the voice of a person — *The Holy Spirit*. All of us in the family of God should hear this voice. We cannot allow ourselves the luxury of being in a hurry or too busy to hear His voice because there is no other voice as important. Let us be attentive. Let us open our ears and our hearts. It is time to prepare our souls to receive because His voice is *Wisdom* itself.

The message of this voice in the desert is: *"Prepare the way for the Lord."* God is a Holy God. The name of His Spirit is precisely, **Holy Spirit**, and the path on which He travels is a holy one. He flows through clean and pure vessels.

> Since we have these promises, dear friends, let us purify
> ourselves from everything that contaminates body and
> spirit, perfecting *holiness* out of reverence for God (*2 Cor.
> 7:1, NIV*).

If we value who Jesus is and the great promises of God
for our lives, we will not allow worldliness to dominate us.
Sins such as *pride, arrogance, bitterness, resentment, lust,* and all
types of *impurity* that contaminate our minds and hearts will
have no place in our lives. We should cleanse ourselves of
these things and prepare the way for a *Holy God.*

Cleansing and Purification

The Scriptures tell of the period of King Hezekiah and
how the Levites were not walking in holiness. One day the
king said unto them: *""Hear me, Levites! Now sanctify yourselves,
sanctify the house of the Lord God of your fathers, and carry out the
rubbish from the holy place." (2 Chr. 29:5).* The command was
three fold and final; *"sanctify now yourselves" "sanctify the house
of the Lord God,"* and *"carry out the rubbish from the holy place".*

The first thing the Levites had to do to be able to minister
was sanctify and purify themselves. In the book of Numbers
we find a description of how they carried out this purification,
and it emphasizes an interesting point.

> In this way, you will set the Levites apart from the rest of
> the people.... After this, they may go in and out of the
> Tabernacle to do their work, because you have purified
> them and presented them as a special offering.... *The Levites
> purified themselves and washed their clothes,* and Aaron

presented them to the Lord as a special offering....From then on the Levites went into the Tabernacle to perform their duties. *(Num. 8:14-16, 21, 22 NLT)*.

Only after being cleansed and purified could they minister, and not before. God had commanded it in that way *(vs. 22)*. Do we put into practice this principle? Are we doing things God's way, or our way? We should be careful to keep the old paths in mind. It is time to stop, look, ask, and return to them *(Jer. 6:16)*. These paths of the past declare that the Levites couldn't minister without being purified.

All this brings me to ask myself, *"In what state am I ministering?" "Am I walking in holiness or in impurity?"*. Yes. God loves weak and broken people; He knows our frame. But **His grace and great compassion are not a license to sin**. The grace of God was manifested to makes us free from sin.

If we want to minister the life of the Holy Spirit, we need to know the path of cleanliness and purity.

In that day a fountain shall be opened for the house of David and for the inhabitants of Jerusalem, for sin and for uncleanness *(Zechariah 13:1)*.

But if we walk in the light, as He is in the light, we have fellowship with one another, and the blood of Jesus Christ His Son cleanse us from all sin....If we confess our sins, He is faithful and just to forgive us ours sins, and to cleanse us from all unrighteousness *(I Jn. 1:7-9)*.

There is a fountain open for the purification of sin and uncleanness. This fountain was opened up at the cross, where the *Lamb of God* was sacrificed for us. Through His sacrifice, and by the power of His blood, we find forgiveness for sins and cleansing for our lives. We need to receive a revelation of Calvary, not just intellectual knowledge of what it is.

Hundreds of books have been written about the work of Redemption. In these pages, I only wish to emphasize that the fountain is flowing today. For the one who repents and turn from his wicked ways, there is forgiveness, cleansing, and freedom in the blood of Jesus.

Falling in Love

Now, you may ask, *"What will empower my heart to live and walk in holiness?"* Good question. You may find strong tendencies toward evil inside of your soul — you are not alone. We are all weak. That's why we need a Savior. We need a Man that can understand our weaknesses and provide divine strength during temptation. That Man is Jesus — He saved us from our sins. Therefore, intimacy with Jesus is the key to walk in holiness.

The more intimate you are with Jesus the more you will fall in love with Him. When you spent time in His presence, gazing at His beauty and majesty, your heart becomes fascinated… captivated… completely lost in the ocean of His love. Then, you will begin to understand that holiness is the expression of His very nature — the nature of the Person you are so in love with.

Humility

We will now observe the importance of walking in humility: *"Every mountain and hill made low…"(Is. 40:4 NLT)*.

Allow me to share part of my testimony. When I was thirteen years old, I played the organ in my father's church in the city of Necochea, in Buenos Aires, Argentina. Rebellion, pride, and arrogance characterized my personality. Like a good teenager, I grew up fully claiming my rights and not respecting anyone, including my parents. In that time,

God spoke to my heart very strongly through a passage in Isaiah. *"The lofty looks of man shall be humbled, the haughtiness of men shall be bowed down, and the Lord alone shall be exalted in that day"* (Is. 2:11). In other words, God told me: *"With those attitudes you aren't going to get anywhere. The haughtiness and arrogance are going to destroy you. Only I am to be exalted in your life, nobody else will take my place."*

It's a tragedy when a prophetic worshiper becomes prideful and arrogant. Not only the one who displays it openly, but also the one that covers his arrogance with a religious niceness, while the reality of his heart is clearly exposed through his attitude and actions.

The Scriptures declare the following:

> Every good gift and every perfect gift is from above, and comes down from the Father of lights.... (*James 1:17*).
> **What makes you better than anyone else?** What do you have that God hasn't given you? And if all you have is from God, why boast as though you have accomplished something on your own? (*1 Cor. 4:7, NLT*).

These verses are clear: *"What makes you better than anyone else? What do you have that God hasn't given you?"* We have received all natural talent and spiritual gifts from God, they are of God, and so there is no reason to feel superior. There are those who are familiar with the Scriptures and know that they have received a certain gift, but they go on acting as if they produced it.

If a prophetic singer or musician is arrogant and prideful, it is because he believes what he has is due to his own merits. He doesn't understand that even the capacity to study an instrument or perfect his voice is God-given.

Descending to the Jordan

In the days of the prophet Elisha, there was a man called *Naaman*, the general of the Syrian army. He needed God not only because he was leprous but because he was prideful. The prophet Elisha sent his servant to *Naaman* with instructions for him to dip himself in the Jordan River seven times so that he would be clean, but *Naaman* did not want to do it.

> But Naaman became furious... and said, "Indeed, I said to myself, `He will surely come out to me, and stand and call on the name of the Lord his God, and wave his hand over the place, and heal the leprosy.' "Are not the Abanah and the Pharpar, the rivers of Damascus, better than all the waters of Israel? Could I not wash in them and be clean?" So he turned and went away in a rage (*2 Kings 5:11-12*).

The great general felt he was far superior to be doing something so low to the point that he wanted to tell God how to heal him. The word Jordan means: *"he who descends, he who lowers himself."* Naaman did not receive God's blessing until he humbled himself.

Sometimes we lose the blessing of God by being very haughty and not lowering and humbling ourselves.

Before beginning His ministry, Jesus Christ descended to the Jordan:

> ....After his baptism, *Jesus came up out of the water, the heavens were opened and he saw the Spirit of God descending* like a dove and settling on him. And a voice from heaven said, "This is my beloved Son..." (*Mt. 3:13-17, NLT*).

Despite being the Son of God, Jesus humbled Himself, descending to the Jordan. And by doing this, the heavens opened and the Holy Spirit descended upon Him. We see a spiritual principle at work here— *"God resists the proud, but gives grace to the humble." (1 Pe. 5:5)*. Another version of the Bible declares: *"...Clothe yourselves in humility in your treatment of one another because "God opposes the proud, but gives grace to the humble"(1 Pe. 5:5, NIV)*. Without the grace of God we will not be able to do anything. If we persist in pride, this grace will not be given unto us, and to complete this shortcoming, God Himself will oppose us. Therefore, we decide what our attitude will be.

A man that God used in this century said the following: *"Always be humble and simple, then God will be able to use you."*

Humility is not an option. One of the keys to walk in this grace is to discover the greatness of our identity in Christ. When we have revelation of who He is and who we are in Him, we will be enabled to walk in true humility. Like Jesus in John 13:1-7, knowing who He was and where He was going, He humble himself, took the towel and washed His disciples' feet.

> For thus says the High and Lofty One who inhabits eternity, whose name is Holy: "I dwell in the high and holy place, with him who has a contrite and humble spirit, to revive the spirit of the humble, and to revive the heart of the contrite ones" *Is. 57:14, 15.*

This passage highlights the two principles we have briefly been dealing with: *Holiness and Humility.* If we walk in this, something will eventually happen in and through us.

> And the glory of the Lord will be revealed, and all mankind together will see it (*Is. 40:5, NIV).*

- To Meditate -

✓ Only after being cleansed and purified could the Levites minister, and not before.

✓ If we want to minister the life of the Holy Spirit, we need to know the path of cleanliness and purity.

✓ The more intimate you are with Jesus the more you will fall in love with Him. When you spent time in His presence, gazing at His beauty and majesty, your heart becomes fascinated... captivated... completely lost in the ocean of His love. Then, you will begin to understand that holiness is the expression of His very nature — the nature of the Person you are so in love with.

✓ If a prophetic worshiper is arrogant and prideful, it is because he believes what he has is due to his own merits. He doesn't understand that even the capacity to study an instrument or perfect his voice is God-given.

✓ One of the keys to walk in humility is to discover the greatness of our identity in Christ. When we have revelation of who He is and who we are in Him, we will be enabled to walk in true humility. Like Jesus in John 13:1-7, knowing who He was and where He was going, He humble himself, took the towel and washed His disciples' feet..

Chapter 8

What Hinders the Flow

Every prophetic worshiper is like a channel through which the river flows. This channel should be clean and free from obstacles so that the river flows easily. Satan is always seeking an obstacle to obstruct the channel. He will do whatever is necessary to distract us and weigh us down with other things because by doing this he will manage to plug our channel. There is something that we should guard continually:

"Keep thy heart with all diligence; for out of it are the issues of life" *(Pr. 4:23, KJV).*

The heart is the center of the human will, that which directs and motivates our thoughts, desires, feelings, values, and decisions. We should guard our heart and occupy it with God. If we do not take responsibility for this, the devil will take charge and invade our soul. When this happens, the heart is obstructed and it closes; life ceases to flow. Quite simply, something or someone has taken the place that only God should have.

There are many forms in which the channel can be obstructed. Usually they are things that we live through, we hear, or we see—circumstances that frequently test us and indicate where we are standing. Our attitude in the face of these trials will determine the condition of our hearts.

Hurdling the Obstacles

As I said before, the devil is a specialist in placing traps to obstruct our channel. He always attempts to distract us and detour us from the plan of God. The greatest error on our part is to fall into the hidden traps that he places. We have to learn to detect and hurdle the obstacles without giving them any importance.

Besides sin and immorality, here are a few things that can become obstructions in the channel and impede the flow of the Spirit in us:

> ➢ *What others think and say about us.*
> ➢ *Unfairness; injustice.*
> ➢ *Disillusion.*
> ➢ *Rejection.*
> ➢ *Bitterness.*

Each of these things has the power to obstruct the channel if we allow entrance into our lives. Situations we live in are often painful. But even these obstacles do not surpass the importance of the life and the flow of God in our hearts. There is nothing or nobody in this world that is worthy of occupying the place that Christ has in our lives. Nothing possesses the sufficient value or the importance that could take priority ahead of Jesus in our soul. There is not even a single valid excuse for us to close our hearts, not even the unjust things that happen to us.

We have to choose between bitterness and God. Bitterness always has a good motive, and it is to be completely fair and just. It is like an opened wound that always remembers what happened. Its strength is that it has good reasoning, but those who embrace bitterness will become one with her and will lose life and the freshness of God.

> ...looking carefully lest anyone fall short of the grace of God; lest any root of bitterness springing up cause trouble, and by this many become defiled (*Heb. 12:15*).

In effect, *bitterness obstructs and contaminates*. Therefore, we should guard our hearts from it if we want the river of God to continue flowing in and through us.

The Path of Love and Forgiveness

Many human dynamics will drive us towards resentment and bitterness. What position will we take? Every day we interact with weak people that offend us in some way. What shall we do? How do we handle those situations? There is only one way — walking in love and forgiveness.

Love covers a multitude of sins. We need a revelation of what God is. God is love, and if we want to act like Him, we have to walk in His love. We need to learn to forgive and love our brothers and sisters, and even our enemies. It is time to grow in the knowledge of His love.

If we cannot forgive, it's because we do not know the love of Christ. Think about this: *When we were worldly sinners that only deserved hell, He chose to love us. Even more, **God knows every mistake that we will make from now to the end, and He still loves us and forgives us**. How will we not love and forgive those who have wounded us, even though they don't deserve it? Wasn't it our rebellion and sin that wounded Christ? What did He do with us? Did He not forgive us and love us?* It is time to reconsider our self-justification and go to the cross. It is only there that we will be able to love and forgive our aggressors. Remember this: *your love for your neighbor is not based on his or her performance toward you. It's based on God's love for you.*

Occasionally, I find myself hindered by something obstructing the flow. In His great mercy, the Holy Spirit illuminates me with His light and reveals the problem. Then, it's up to me to stay down below lamenting over my wound, or to deny myself, go to the cross and forgive. *It is only when I decide to love and forgive that I can return to flow in Him.*

More Obstacles to Overcome

There are many other things that hinder the flow of the Spirit trough us, for example:

> ➢ *Envy.*
> ➢ *Competing with others.*
> ➢ *Selfish ambition to obtain a position whatever the cost.*
> ➢ *Jealousy.*
> ➢ *Strife.*
> ➢ *Impure motives.*
> ➢ *Unbelief, etc.*

We should guard our hearts from all of these because we can easily fall into these sins. *Nothing should separate our hearts from Jesus.* In the moment that something else takes His place, we are in danger. We should be careful and continually depend on God in prayer.

The Path of Wisdom

> When wisdom enters your heart, and knowledge is pleasant to your soul, discretion will preserve you; understanding will keep you, to deliver you from the way of evil.... (Pr. 2:10-12).

We will be free from the evil path when the wisdom of God directs us. His intelligence will save us from the traps of the devil and His wisdom will make us sharp, prudent, and precautious. Wisdom will teach us that the way to the continuous flow of God in our lives is having an intimate and daily relationship with Him. Intimacy will keep our channel open and clean.

Let us not become careless with this point. Just because our channel is not obstructed today doesn't mean that it won't be tomorrow. Above everything that we guard, let us guard our heart.

- To Meditate -

✓ There is nothing or nobody in this world that is worthy of occupying the place that Christ has in our lives.

✓ Nothing possesses the sufficient value or the importance that could take priority ahead of Jesus in our soul.

✓ Love covers a multitude of sins. We need a revelation of what God is. God is love, and if we want to act like Him, we have to walk in His love. We need to learn to forgive and love our brothers and sisters, and even our enemies. It is time to grow in the knowledge of His love.

✓ Remember this: *your love for your neighbor is not based on his or her performance toward you. It's based on God's love for you..*

✓ The secret to the continuous flow of God in our lives is having an intimate and daily relationship with Him.

Chapter 9

Be Careful That You Don't Fall!

The Bible relates the story of a man who experienced the power and the Presence of the Most High from childhood. He was an excellent musician, a man of war, and a king without precedent. But one day, when he found himself at the pinnacle of his ministry, he began to belittle God and despise the anointing of the Holy Spirit that was upon him. *This man was David, the sweet psalmist of Israel.*

It happened in the spring of the year, at the time when kings go out to battle, that David sent Joab and his servants with him, and all Israel; and they destroyed the people of Ammon and besieged Rabbah. But David remained at Jerusalem (*2 Sam. 11:1*).

David's first mistake was to forget his responsibilities. It was the time in which the kings went out to war, but he stayed in Jerusalem. He should have been directing the soldiers in the battle. Perhaps David's argument was: *"So many years have passed that I have been going out to war. I have bathed my sword in blood many times. I believe it is now time for me to stay at home and rest in my palace and let someone else do the job. God has given me countless victories, and I am a successful king. What more could I want? I think my staying at home is quite justified, and I can give orders from here without even leaving. I am tired of doing the same thing. I want to enjoy my success a bit, and I am going to do that by staying here in Jerusalem. Besides, I think I deserve it, right?"* David made a mistake in staying because his idleness opened the door to the devil and here began his moral ruin.

The Lord has determined a specific purpose for each of us, a destiny that we should reach. *(If you still don't know what yours is, seek God and ask Him. You are not on this earth by accident. You are a person with purpose).*

Whatever the objective is, our responsibility is to work towards the goal. As we will see later on, laziness and idleness are the first link of a chain that descends to natural and spiritual ruin.

I went by the field of the lazy man, And by the vineyard of the man devoid of understanding; and there it was, all overgrown with thorns; its surface was covered with nettles; its stone wall was broken down. When I saw it, I considered it well; I looked on it and received instruction.... *(Pr. 24:30–32).*

This passage draws a picture of laziness and irresponsibility. It shows us the importance of daily caring, cultivating and protecting our vineyard — *as we saw in the previous chapter* — the importance of guarding our hearts.

Let us not be lazy, nor lack understanding; let us not allow thorns to grow in our lives. Maintain the stone-wall without holes through which the enemy could enter. Look at what happened to David and be warned.

The Danger of Not Guarding our Eyes

> Then it happened one evening that David arose from his
> bed and walked on the roof of the king's house. And from
> the roof he saw a woman bathing, and the woman was
> very beautiful to behold (*2 Sam. 11:2*).

David rose from his sleep, but not at the time when men
go to work. He arose in the early evening and began to walk
about because he did not have anything better to do. It was
as if he was waiting for something, and the devil was in charge
of giving it to him. *"He saw a woman bathing, and the woman
was very beautiful to behold"* (*2 Sam.11:2*). Now, in order for
David to know that Bathsheba was beautiful, he had to have
observed her very carefully; and in order for him to covet
her in his heart, he must have observed her quite well and
for a long time.

We should be very careful with our eyes; we cannot
allow them to see just anything.

> Your eye is a lamp for your body. *A pure eye* lets sunshine
> into your soul. But *an evil eye* shuts out the light and plunges
> you into darkness. (*Luke 11:34, NLT*).

The following events that occurred in David's life were
a direct result of not keeping his eyes on the Beautiful One,
God. He was no longer directing his thirst and desire toward
the Lord. No longer was he satisfied with Jehovah. His eye
became malignant and placed his body in darkness. He first
gave in to laziness and left the door open to lust.
Lasciviousness ignited through the eyes, and he could not be
stopped at that point.

Every human being, starting with me, runs the risk of falling into this sin, even more those who follow God like David did. If we do not learn to find our satisfaction in God and guard our eyes from evil, we will have countless problems.

We should do something about it!

"I made a covenant with my eyes not to look with lust upon a young woman" (Job 31:1 NLT).

Job made a covenant with his eyes in order to evade the impure desires that arose when he looked with lust at a young woman. He knew that he was weak. Job wanted to please God, and for this reason, he guarded his eyes.

If this kind of danger existed in the time of Job, how much more does it exist in our day? Today, as our technology increases, this trap is set everywhere. We should make a covenant with our eyes, put on the brakes, and not allow ourselves to gaze at the things that are not convenient for us.

You know the next commandment pretty well, too: 'Don't go to bed with another's spouse.' But don't think you've preserved your virtue simply by staying out of bed. Your *heart* can be corrupted by lust even quicker than your *body*. Those leering looks you think nobody notices—thy also corrupt- (Mt. 5:27-28, The Message).

There are different types of looking. Jesus was not referring to simply looking at a woman, but rather looking her with lust. I consider that is acceptable to acknowledge beauty in the opposite sex, but we must move on immediately in our thoughts toward the Lord, re-focusing our eyes on the beauty of God. The prophetic worshiper's eye is vital- *that's why our enemy will always try to corrupt it with lust*. Keep in mind that lust is the ultimate counterfeit of God's love.

The best lust-empowered tool that Satan has today is pornography. Sadly, with the help of technology millions are been swept by it—unbelievers and believers.

If you have a problem with pornography and are willing to repent, know that God deeply loves you and want to set you free. He desires to fill your heart with holy passion. Turn to Him. Quit filling your eyes with immorality and start saturating your gaze with Jesus and His beauty. There are three excellent books that I believe will help you. *"Wild at Heart"* and *"The Journey of Desire"*, by John Eldredge. Also, *"After God's Own Heart"* by Mike Bickle.

So, what was the downfall of David? Well, he gazed at Bathsheba with intense lust, and this led him to covet her. From there an immoral desire was produced, an inordinate passion, one that he could not resist. When he had the opportunity, he consummated it. This is precisely what Job feared. He knew the desires were going to arise, and for this reason made a covenant with his eyes. Sadly, David did not understand it that way, and the Scriptures were fulfilled:

> But each one is tempted when he is drawn away by his own desires and enticed. Then, when desire has conceived, it gives birth to sin; and sin, when it is full-grown, brings forth death. (*James 1:14, 15*).

The Process of Sin

> So David sent and inquired about the woman... "Is this not Bathsheba... the wife of Uriah the Hittite?" Then David sent messengers, and took her; and she came to him, and he lay with her" (*2 Sam. 11:3-4*).

It is here where the process of sin is accomplished, in the same form that it was accomplished by Adam and Eve in the Garden of *Eden (Gen. 5: 6): seeing, coveting, taking, and eating.* It did not matter to David that the woman was already married; the sin process was burning inside of him and had blinded him. For this reason, it was so easy for him to commit adultery and later kill. The best form of impeding this process is to cut it off in the beginning, at the first sight of it; then there will be no chance for it to grow.

Do we realize the importance of making a covenant with our eyes? One day the prophet Isaiah asked, *"Who among us shall dwell with the devouring fire? Who among us shall dwell with everlasting burnings?* And among other things he responds: *"He who...shuts his eyes from seeing evil: He will dwell on high...Your eyes will see the King in His beauty"* (Is. 33:15-16). Isn't this a great and glories deal? **If we shut our eyes from seeing evil we will see King Jesus in His Beauty**. This is our birthright and our eternal reward — *To behold the beauty of our King.*

The Power of the Life-Giving Spirit

If you say, *"I have tried to guard my eyes, but I can't. I find in myself a very strong tendency to do that which is prohibited, and actually do it,"* If you sincerely want to change, don't be afraid! There is hope in Jesus! If you are a child of God, I want to remind you who lives inside of you — the *Holy Spirit.* Your tendencies and inclinations toward evil can be strong, but the *Law* of the Spirit of Life is greater and stronger, and it has overcome the *law* of sin and of death. If you present yourself before God every day, as a living sacrifice *(Rom. 12:1),* and spend time worshiping and falling in love with Jesus, you will discover how the powerful law of the Spirit begins to regulate and activate your entire being.

He that lives in you is greater than he that is in the world, and His nature is stronger than yours. Just cling to Him and trust in His power.

One Thing Leads To Another

Summing up this sad stage in David's life, Bathsheba ended up pregnant, and the king sent for her husband, Uriah, who was on the front line of the battle. The plan was for him to go to his house and sleep with his wife, but Uriah turned out to be a more righteous man than David and did not want to rest. So, seeing that the king could not cover his sin with deceit, he decided to commit murder.

> And he wrote in the letter, saying, "Set Uriah in the forefront of the hottest battle, and retreat from him, that he may be struck down and die" *(2 Sam. 11:15).*

And to think that this all began because David did not do what he was supposed to. First, it was his *laziness* to go off to war. Next, he gave in to *lust* and *covetousness*, followed by *adultery* along with *lies* and *deceit*. Finally, he committed *homicide*.

How is it possible that this could happen to the sweet psalmist of Israel? Well, I believe that in his early years, persecution by his enemies forced him to depend on God. The anguish and pain brought his heart back to God time after time. But when this pressure ended and prosperity arrived, David found himself very sure and firm. Without having a necessity for God, that which had been hidden in his heart came to the light.

Examining Our Hearts

If we were in David's position, with his authority, power, and dominion, can we assure ourselves that we would not do the same thing? Often I have heard the following comment: *"Power or a position of authority changes a person."* On the contrary, I think that instead of changing them it brings out their reality.

The same potential for sin that was in David is in us. It is for this reason that we continually need Jesus, in our failures as well as in our successes, in the good times and bad. We never have to trust in ourselves but should only lean on and trust in God. *(Jer. 17:9, 10/Pr. 28:26).*

Trust in the Lord with all your heart, and lean not on your own understanding; in all your ways acknowledge Him, And He shall direct your paths. Do not be wise in your own eyes; Fear the Lord and depart from evil (Pr. 3:5-7).

The man who knows what he is capable of doing will develop a trust and dependence in the Lord.

David Despised God

The word of God indicates: *"But the thing that David had done displeased the Lord"* (2 Sam. 11:27). About one year passed between the time of David's sin and God's orders to the prophet Nathan to go and reprimand him. It was as if the Lord was waiting for David to repent on his own. Nevertheless, the heart of the king was hard because of the deceit of sin *(Heb. 3:13).* But there came a day in which God made him realize what he had actually done.

Then Nathan said to David...Thus says the Lord God of Israel: 'I anointed you king over Israel, and I delivered you from the hand of Saul. I gave you your master's house and your master's wives into your keeping, and gave you the house of Israel and Judah. And if that had been too little, I also would have given you much more! Why have you despised the commandment of the Lord, to do evil in His sight? You have killed Uriah...you have taken his wife to be your wife... 'Now therefore, the sword shall never depart from your house, **because you have despised Me**, and have taken the wife of Uriah the Hittite to be your wife.' *(2 Sam. 12:7-10)*.

The first thing God mentions is: *"I anointed you,"* as if reminding him of the immense value of the anointing that had been poured out upon him, and what he had despised. Not only this, but God also freed David from his enemies, poured out blessings upon his life, and much more. But David belittled the word of God, and the Lord himself said unto David: *"you have despised me."* In the original Hebrew this word *"bazah"* means to *not esteem or to treat with disrespect, to make fun of.* David despised God, he did not esteem Him, and he made fun of Him to His face.

The Consequences of Sin

But *you have given the enemies of the Lord great opportunity* to despise and blaspheme him, so your child will die *(2 Sam. 12:14 NLT)*.

In this stage of his life, David represents those ministers that bring shame to the gospel and give the enemies of the Lord an opportunity to blaspheme Him because of their actions.

The good thing is that when the prophet reprimanded David, he recognized his sin. Psalm fifty-one shows David's repentance. But even though God forgave David his sins, He did not free him from the natural consequences. David *knew God and had spiritual authority.* The consequences of despising the Lord were fatal. The son that Bathsheba gave him died. Other of David's children became immoral and assassins like him. His daughter, Tamar, and her   concubines were raped by two of his sons, Amnon and Absalom *(2 Sam. 13:14/ 16:22).*

Absalom also assassinated his brother Amnon *(2 Sam. 13:28),* and then rose up against his father, trying to take away his kingdom *(2 Sam. 15).* Absalom was finally killed by Joab *(2 Sam. 18:9-17).* Another of David's sons, Adonias, also rebelled by usurping the throne and was executed *(2 Sam.12:10-12).* David's life was stained forever. He suffered the consequences of sin for the rest of his life.

The Most Important Part

David ended up returning to God and pleading for His mercy. One of the things he prayed was: *"Do not cast me away from Your presence, and do not take Your Holy Spirit from me" (Ps. 51:11).* Once again he straightened out his priorities. Now, more than ever, David realized what was most important in his life. It wasn't his army, his kingdom, not even his own life. The most valuable thing that David possessed was the Presence of God and the fellowship of the Holy Spirit.

A Call to Attention

Prophetic worshipers: let us have a lifestyle of gazing upon the Glorious One. Let's labor to keep our eyes and hearts captured by the beauty of the Man Christ Jesus—that our affections may burn only for Him.

We can learn much from David's mistakes—the sweet psalmist of Israel. Listen carefully to the following words of Paul:

> These things happened to them as examples and were written down as warnings for us, on whom the fulfillment of the ages has come. *So, if you think you are standing firm, be careful that you don't fall! (1Cor.10:11-12, NIV).*

In the coming chapter, we will study how we can develop a lifestyle of gazing upon the Glorious One.

- To Meditate -

✓ Laziness and idleness are the first links of a chain that descends to natural and spiritual ruin.

✓ The process of sin is *seeing, coveting, taking, and eating.*

✓ The prophetic worshiper's eye is vital- *that's why our enemy will always try to corrupt it with lust.*

✓ If you present yourself before God every day as a living sacrifice *(Rom. 12:1)* and spend time worshiping and falling in love with Jesus, you will discover how the powerful law of the Spirit begins to regulate and activate your entire being.

✓ *Prophetic worshipers:* Let us have a lifestyle of gazing upon the Glorious One. Let's labor to keep our eyes and hearts captured by the beauty of the Man Christ Jesus — that our affections may burn only for Him.

Chapter 10

Prayer and Fasting

The generation of prophetic worshipers that the Lord is raising up is a group of people that will live a lifestyle of prayer and fasting.

Prayer and fasting are spiritual disciplines that anyone who desires to grow in the knowledge of God has to practice. The person that gives himself to these disciplines will encounter more of the burning heart of God and discover the joy of His presence. Then, the thrill of encountering God will be the motive for doing the disciplines. He or she will start praying and fasting out of the pleasure of knowing Him, not out of duty or obligation.

The sweet psalmist of Israel declared this: *"One thing I have desired of the Lord, that will I seek, that I may dwell in the house of the Lord all the days of my life, to behold the beauty of the Lord and to inquire in His temple"* (Ps. 27:4). David also sang about the fullness of joy that is found in God's presence and about the everlasting pleasures that are at His right hand (Ps. 16:11). Not only that, but He came to know the river of God's pleasures (Ps. 36:8).

Now, why David used such extreme words to describe his experience with God? As we can notice, he was not seeking the Lord out of duty. Nobody had to convince him to go to pray. Intimacy with the Lord was the joy of his life.

The transcendent realms of the knowledge of God that David touched are available for us today. Yes. And we can access them through prayer and fasting. Put differently, through prayer and fasting we position our hearts for encounter. We deny ourselves of other things to focus on "one thing", the very "one thing" that David was obsessed with — the beauty of God.

After reading this, it's normal for some of you to be thinking, *"Well, to be honest I find prayer really boring, though I believe at some point can become enjoyable. But fasting? What pleasure can you find in fasting?"* Actually, you can find pleasure in fasting. But I am not talking about carnal pleasure.

For example, fasting food can be really hard on our flesh, yet, in the economy of God is one of the best ways of denying inferior pleasures to break into eternal ones. Fasting it's a spiritual discipline that accelerates the process of receiving revelation from heaven. When we do it, our hearts get tenderized and we see and hear God more clearly.

Would you like to experience more of God and more often? Add fasting to your prayer life. Fasting positions our hearts to receive more from God and more quickly.

Receiving Divine Strength

"That He would grant you, according to the riches of His glory, to be strengthened with might through His Spirit in the inner man" *(Eph. 3:16).* "Be strong in the Lord and in the power of His might" (Eph. 6:10).

Through fasting we offer our strength to receive God's. We say no to human strength to receive divine might. In the grace of God, we deny ourselves of legitimately pleasures like eating, entertainment, etc. to pursue the Lord harder. By doing it, our focus on the Lord grows and we become mighty in spirit, mighty inside. Even though fasting weakens our flesh, our inner man grows stronger.

"...increasing in the knowledge of God; strengthened with all might, according to His glorious power, for all patience and longsuffering with joy" (Col. 1:10-11).

We need divine might to attain patience and perseverance, and we need patience and perseverance to resist the attacks from demons and evil people toward us. It is the might of God that enables us to patiently endure and resist temptation and evil every day. In order to have victory over darkness we must daily receive power from on high. By having lifestyles of prayer and fasting we position ourselves to receive an ongoing flow of divine strength.

On the other hand, if we choose not to have a lifestyle of prayer and fasting we will be weak as others men are. Yes, sincerely loving the Lord but with very weak minds and hearts; prompt to fall in temptation, depression and boredom.

I am convinced that in order to face the present assault of darkness against us, and the increasing manifestation of evil at the end of the age, we need to receive all the might and grace that God can gives us. A lifestyle of prayer and fasting provides the platform for this to occur.

Spending our Time and Energy Wisely

"Why do you spend money for what is not bread, and your wages for what does not satisfy? Listen carefully to me, and eat what is good, and let your soul delight itself in abundance. Incline your ear, and come to Me. Hear, and your soul shall live..." (Is. 55:2-3).

Money represents our time and energy. I believe that one of the things that the Lord is highlighting in the passage above is the way we steward our affections. Plain and clearly He is asking, *why are you spending your time, money and energy in what does not satisfy?*

Time after time, I found myself distracted and bother by many things. Spending my time and energy in activities that are not necessarily sinful (because the stuff is usually legitimate and good), but the problem is that steals my time away from the most important things. Graciously, the Holy Spirit calls my attention and reminds me of the only thing that can satisfy my heart—Jesus.

It takes violence and determination to keep the flame of our hearts burning for God. It will not happen by accident. Each day we must fight to stay focus on the things that matter for eternity.

In our present age, we have many ways of getting distracted. Too many options available. The question arises, how do we stay focus on the Lord while living in the midst of an ocean of alternatives? It's not ease, but not impossible. Fasting helps us to stay focus on God.

A fasted lifestyle removes our options in a consistent way and eliminates the usual "props" that we lean on *(entertainment, eating, sports, movies, relationships, etc)*. As I said before, many of those activities are good and legitimate. The problem is, that we often use them in excess and have a talent to hide behind them. Yes, we humans like to hide, just like our ancestors Adam and Eve. Also, we lean on our props because they bring a temporary relief to the pain of our hearts. Our props are false comforts. The truth is, that there is only One that can heal the wound of our souls—our Maker. We were made for God, to love Him and be loved by Him.

A lifestyle of prayer and fasting facilitates the unfolding of knowledge of God to our hearts. By embracing this way of living, we violently remove the props and consistently set ourselves in front of the changing-fire of God's heart.

Prayer and fasting help us to spend our time and energy on the "one thing" David desired. We learn to wait before the Lord and to hear His voice. We go deep into the study and the meditation of God's Word, coming to eat what is good — the bread of life.

It is wise to ask ourselves every morning, who will be the recipient of my time and energy today? Who will be the object of my affections, God or the idols of this world? Whether we like it or not, we must face the reality that our affections will burn for something or someone; the question is, what or who? Who will be the primary object of my affections?

As we willingly choose God every day, He will help us in our weaknesses and empower our hearts to go hard after Him.

Longing for the Presence of the Bridegroom

> Then John's disciples came and asked him, "How is that we and the Pharisees fast, but your disciples do not fast?" Jesus answered, "How can the guests of the bridegroom mourn while he is with them? The time will come when the bridegroom will be taken from them, **then they will fast**." Matt. 9:14-15, NIV

The primary longing of a prophetic worshiper should be the manifest presence of Jesus, our heavenly Bridegroom. We pray and fast as an expression of our longing for Him. Prayer and fasting are the on-ramps we use to express and develop our deep desire to see His glory and kingdom revealed on earth.

In his book *"After God's Own Heart"*, Mike Bickle brilliantly explains the power of the Bridegroom Fast:

"Fasting has very powerful rewards that are primarily internal, aimed at the human heart. The fast of the Old Testament was mostly for external purposes, but the Bridegroom fast touches the heart. It has a different focus. As we pursue the Lord by the grace of God through the Bridegroom fast, our physical appetites, emotional appetites, and spiritual appetites change dramatically. In a word, we gain more desire. He imparts new desires of delight to us so that fasting is not drudgery but an indescribable privilege because it brings us closer to Him and His delight for us. There is nothing the human spirit craves more than to enter into these delights, but most people don't know they exist. The lifestyle of fasting is rare, and so the benefits are rare. Not only is there the impartation of new desires, but also there is the removal or diminution of sinful desires. Beloved, when our desires line up properly, life is wonderful. When our desires are out of line, life is burdensome. Fasting, rather than increasing life's drudgery, actually releases supernatural joy. The Old Testament fast was related so often to suffering, to the affliction of our body, to the affliction of our soul. That paradigm has taken root in church history. People fast to "pay the price." But I tell you there is a pleasure in fasting—and many rewards. You can very quickly grow to love fasting. You actually lament interruptions that prevent you from continuing in it for a time. I get into the rhythm of the kind of fasting I have engaged in for the last couple of years, and when something interrupts it, I never think, *Good, I can take a break.Where's the all-you-can-eat buffet?* Just the opposite—I want to return to fasting as quickly as God will allow. You will find that the hunger to experience God begins to dominate your life. It's a strange paradox that we actually hunger to fast. I believe it is going to be a common experience to love fasting. It will take some time, but in the long run this is how the body of Christ will choose to live"

We are invited to taste and see that the Lord is good. As we rapidly approach the end of the age, the unfolding of the knowledge of God to this generation will be unprecedented. We still don't have a mindset to comprehend the dimensions of glory and trouble that are before us. Therefore, now is the time to get our hearts in position to receive from heaven. It is through prayer and fasting that we can take a hold of that which God has ordained for us.

Dear reader, there is divine grace and might available for you. You only have to say yes. Not matter how weak and broken you may feel—dare to embrace a lifestyle of prayer and fasting. As you do, watch how the Holy Spirit empowers your heart with holy and fiery desires, and how He anoints your eyes with revelation and fills your soul with His consuming Love.

Today is the day. Taste and see that the Lord is good!

- To Meditate -

✓ The generation of prophetic worshipers that the Lord is raising up is a group of people that will live a lifestyle of prayer and fasting.

✓ Fasting it's a spiritual discipline that accelerates the process of receiving revelation from heaven. When we do it, our hearts get tenderized and we see and hear God more clearly.

✓ By having lifestyles of prayer and fasting we position ourselves to receive an ongoing flow of divine strength.

✓ In order to face the present assault of darkness against us, and the increasing manifestation of evil at the end of the age, we need to receive all the might and grace that God can gives us. A lifestyle of prayer and fasting provides the platform for this to occur.

✓ The primary longing of a prophetic worshiper should be the manifest presence of Jesus, our heavenly Bridegroom. We pray and fast as an expression of our longing for Him. Prayer and fasting are the on-ramps we use to express and develop our deep desire to see His glory and kingdom revealed on earth.

Chapter 11

Growing in Intimacy

In these last two chapters, I will focus on the importance of living in intimate communion with Jesus. The most important thing in the life of a prophetic worshiper is to grow in love and intimacy with God.

There are various levels of communion; some are superficial, and others go deeper. Let's observe three different people that were with and knew Jesus on different levels.

> Jesus came to Bethany, where Lazarus was who had been dead, whom He had raised from the dead. There they made Him a supper; and Martha served, but Lazarus was one of those who sat at the table with Him. Then Mary took a pound of very costly oil of spikenard, anointed the feet of Jesus, and wiped His feet with her hair. And the house was filled with the fragrance of the oil *(Jn. 12:1-3)*.

These three people that I am referring to are *Martha, Lazarus, and Mary*. Martha served, Lazarus was banqueting with Jesus, and Mary was at His feet. The three were with Jesus, but they were all in different places.

Martha: Serving the Master

Martha is always seen serving, which is good, but she worried so much about her service that it took the place of the most important thing.

But Martha was distracted by all the preparations that had to be made. She came to him and asked, "Lord, don't you care that my sister has left me to do the work by myself? Tell her to help me!" *"Martha, Martha,"* the Lord answered, *"you are worried and upset about many things, but only one thing is needed. Mary has chosen what is better,* and it will not be taken away from her" *(Lk. 10:40-42, NIV).*

Martha had a problem with her priorities. She considered what she was doing to be the most important thing and began to judge her sister *(who saw things differently)* as wasting her time. Then Jesus explained to Martha what should be in first place.

Our service to God is important, but it is not the most important thing because we end up running the risk of serving a God that we don't even know.

The relationship that Martha had with Jesus was not the same as her sister's. This was very evident when Lazarus died. *"Then Martha said to Jesus, "Lord, if You had been here, my brother would not have died. " (Jn. 11:21) "Then, when Mary came where Jesus was, and saw Him, she fell down at His feet, saying to Him, "Lord, if You had been here, my brother would not have died."(Jn. 11:32).* Both Martha and Mary said the same thing to Jesus, but Jesus reacted very differently to each. Martha heard that Jesus was coming and went out to meet Him *(v. 20).* When she was before Him, the first thing that she did was protest His late arrival. On the other hand, when Mary heard that Jesus had called for her, she arose quickly and ran to Him.

When she arrived in His presence, the first thing she did was to see Him *(v. 32)*. There is no record of whether Martha stopped to look at Him. She came before Jesus and immediately opened her mouth. Mary had the ability to see Jesus, but Martha did not. After seeing Him, the same verse says that Mary *"fell down at His feet"* (something that Martha never did) and spoke the same words as her sister, but the reaction was different. *"When Jesus saw her weeping... He groaned in the spirit and was troubled."* *(Jn. 11:33)*. Why didn't Jesus respond this way with Martha? Didn't she say the same thing as Mary? The words were the same, but the relationship was different. The relationship that Martha had with Jesus was cold and intellectual. Mary, on the other hand, knew the Master's affections for her and how to touch His heart.

Lazarus: Banqueting with the King

> There they made Him a supper; and Martha served, but Lazarus was one of those who sat at the table with Him *(Jn. 12:2)*.

He who had risen from the dead was now feasting at the table with Jesus. Lazarus represents those who sit at the table and dine with the King. *'Behold, I stand at the door and knock. If anyone hears My voice and opens the door, I will come in to him and dine with him, and he with Me' (Rev. 3:20)*. These are the people who hear the call of the Lord on a deeper level. They open the door of their hearts and enter into closer communion with Him.

In the book of Song of Solomon, the Shulamite brilliantly describes this level of intimacy:

> *"He brought me to the banqueting house, and his banner over me was love"(S. S. 2:3, 4)*.

Is in this house that we discover the deep affections of God's heart for us. Our eyes become enlightened and we begin to understand the glories riches of being Jesus' inheritance (Eph. 1:18). This is a fantastic place — life changing. As we are engulfed by God's affections we begin to feel the burning desire of His heart for us. Then, the Holy Spirit persuades our hearts that God's banner over us is love. In other words, the heavenly statement over our lives; God's point of view; His confession over us — is love. Isn't this wonderful? Isn't this what our hearts long for, to be truly loved and desired?

Undoubtedly, this is the deep longing of every human being. We were created to love and be loved by Him. God's affections define who we are. Our identity is based on the fact that we are loved and desired by Him. Of course, our un-renewed minds and those around us will offer different definitions of who we are. But only one opinion counts now and for eternity — God's.

Dear reader, allow the Holy Spirit to take you to the banqueting house. I promise — you will never be the same

Everyone who thirsts, Come to the waters; and you who have no money, Come, buy and eat. Yes, come; buy wine and milk without money and without price. Why do you spend money for what is not bread, and your wages for what does not satisfy? *Listen carefully to Me, and eat what is good, And let your soul delight itself in abundance. Incline your ear, and come to Me. Hear, and your soul shall live* (Is. 55:1-3).

Mary: At His Feet

Mary went even deeper in her relationship with Jesus. *"...And Mary sat at Jesus' feet and heard His word" (Lk. 10:39.KJ)*. She took the time to hear the words of His mouth. If she had been doing something else, it would have been very difficult to hear the voice of the Teacher. Mary set apart time for the most important thing — *to know Him*.

> Then Mary took a pound of very costly oil of spikenard, anointed the feet of Jesus, and wiped His feet with her hair. And the house was filled with the fragrance of the oil *(Jn. 12:3)*.

If you study Mary's life you will find out that she was severely criticized. Her extreme devotion was offensive to many. People were disrupted by her extravagant love. But Jesus honored her passion and praised the wisdom of her choices. The beauty of the Master captured Mary's heart in such a way that she offered the most precious thing she had. This spikenard perfume was very costly, representing precisely one year's salary. She took this perfume and poured it out on the feet of her beloved as an act of adoration, love, and surrender.

Mary's extreme devotion demonstrated where her greatest treasure was. As the Lord said, *"For where your treasure is, there your heart will also be" (Mt. 6:21)*. Her heart was with Jesus. He was her greatest reward. That's why she was able to give away her most precious possession.

It's interesting to notice that, our treasure will be the object of our worship. A good question to ask would be, *"who or what is my treasure?"* We need to be very careful so that we do not end up offering our worship to something or someone that is not God.

The wisdom of Mary was to choose the only necessary thing — *intimacy with Jesus*. She came to know Him in a deeper way because she made Him the magnificent obsession of her life.

By the time Jesus was going to the cross, Mary was so in love with Him, so captured by His beauty that no sacrifice seemed to great. *What was the amount of one's year salary compared to this Man?* He was God made flesh, the maker of heaven and earth, the owner and author of all creation. She seized the moment, gave her heart away and filled the house with the fragrance of her extravagant worship.

Dear reader, the invitation to intimately know the Lord is open. He wants you to come closer. Let's grow in the knowledge of Him. Let's have a lifestyle of gazing upon His beauty.

I would like to end this book looking at the life of Ruth — *A Martha who also was Lazarus and Mary.*

- To Meditate -

✓ Our service to God is important, but it is not the most important thing *because we end up running the risk of serving a God that we don't even know.*

✓ The banqueting house is a place of fellowship and revelation, where we learn to feast and celebrate on God's abundant mercy and goodness. We grow in the knowledge of His love and come to experience the pleasures of being loved by Him.

✓ God's affections define who we are. Our identity is based on the fact that we are loved and desired by Him.

✓ The wisdom of Mary was to choose the only necessary thing—*intimacy with Jesus.* She came to know Him in a deeper way because she made Him the magnificent obsession of her life.

Chapter 12

Knowing Jesus

Getting to know Jesus is a process. As we live and walk with Him, the Holy Spirit will expand and enlarge our understanding of His person and how important we are to Him.

There is a beautiful picture of this process in the Old Testament—the story of Ruth.

As you may know, *Naomi, Ruth's mother-in-law*, had lost her husband and her two sons in the country of Moab. As a result, Naomi decided to return to her homeland, Judah. Her two daughters-in-law wanted to go to Judah with Naomi, but she suggested they return to their mothers' houses. One agreed, but the other insisted upon staying with her mother-in-law.

And she said, "Look, your sister-in-law has gone back to her people and to her gods; return after your sister-in-law." But Ruth said: "Entreat me not to leave you, or to turn back from following after you; For wherever you go, I will go; and wherever you lodge, I will lodge; Your people shall be my people, And your God, my God. Where you die, I will die, and there will I be buried. The Lord do so to

me, and more also, If anything but death parts you and
me." *(Ruth 1:15-17).*

Ruth was determined to follow *Naomi,* whatever the cost;
she wasn't going to turn back. There was something deep
within Ruth's heart that told her that she would change
forever in Judah, and that is just what happened.

Leaving the Country of Moab

So Naomi returned, and Ruth the Moabitess her daughter-
in-law with her, who returned from the country of Moab.
(Ruth 1:22).

The first step that Ruth took was to leave Moab in order
to enter into Israel. In the same way, when we receive the
Lord Jesus Christ into our hearts, we change ruler and
kingdom. *(Col. 1:13).* This is proven through true repentance
like Ruth's. She turned around *one-hundred and eighty* degrees,
abandoned the fields of Moab and never returned. Her
progress in God began with this decision.

Receiving Jesus as our Lord is only the beginning; from
there on out, we should grow in the grace and the knowledge
of our Savior *(2 Pt. 3:18).*

Types and Shadows

Before continuing, I would like to observe the names of
the people in the book of Ruth because they typify spiritual
persons. Let us look at four of these names:

> ➢ **Boaz** — *Typifies Christ*
> ➢ **Ruth** — *Typifies the Church, the Bride of Christ.*

> ➤ **Naomi** — *In the second period of her life, I consider her a poetic parallel of the Holy Spirit. She was the one to guide Ruth and instruct her into a deeper communion with Boaz, her redeemer.*

> ➤ **The reapers** — *Typify the anointed ones of God*

The Field Of Boaz

So Ruth... said to Naomi, "Please let me go to the field, and glean heads of grain after him in whose sight I may find favor." And she said to her, "Go, my daughter." Then she left, and went and gleaned in the field after the reapers. And she happened to come to the part of the field belonging to Boaz, who was of the family of Elimelech- *Ruth 2:2, 3.*

Ruth was not satisfied with merely entering into Judah, she sought to do something useful and so began to glean in the fields of Boaz.

Then Boaz said to his servant who was in charge of the reapers, "Whose young woman is this?" So the servant... said, "It is the young Moabite woman who came back with Naomi from the country of Moab." And she said, 'Please let me glean and gather after the reapers among the sheaves.' So she came and has continued from morning until now...." *(Ruth 2:5-7).*

Ruth didn't pay attention to who the owner of the field was; she only knew that there was abundance therein. She gleaned what the others left and filled her hands with food, supplying her needs in that way.

Like the field of Boaz, the kingdom of God is full of blessings. Everything that we need is there. Often we lose blessings because we don't work gleaning and gathering as Ruth did. *On the other hand,* it is interesting to see that we can have the blessings of the kingdom without knowing the King. We shouldn't be satisfied with the gleanings. If the blessings are beautiful, how much more is He who gives them? We need to find the owner of the field and form a relationship with Him.

The First Encounter

Then Boaz said to Ruth, "You will listen, my daughter, will you not? Do not go to glean in another field, nor go from here, but stay close…"Let your eyes be on the field which they reap, and go after them….And when you are thirsty, go to the vessels and drink from what the young men have drawn." *(Ruth 2:8, 9).*

Paraphrasing this passage, Boaz told Ruth: *"This field is the best place for you to be. Come and gather all your food here, and don't go anywhere else to seek it. I am happy to have you here. Don't seek any other source to supply your needs, nor return unto Moab – stay here in my field."*

Another thing Boaz told Ruth during their first encounter was for her to stay close by his maidens *(reapers —* that she should look where they gleaned and go after them. When she was thirsty, she was to go unto the vessels and drink the water that the young men had drawn. If Ruth had tried to gather by herself, she would have lost the best field, and perhaps would have died of hunger *(Ruth 2:15-16).*

The reapers typify the anointed ones of God. His advice is that we *"stay close to them and follow them."* God has placed anointed ministers over us. We should stay close to them during the season God leads, honor them, and follow them.

Seeking Your Own Spring

I know ministers who are like springs in the middle of the desert. No matter where they are, powerful waters flow from within them and impart life to everyone around them. This is possible because they have their own spring. Ruth, at this time, did not have a spring. She depended upon the servants to live.

Is this our case? Certainly we must drink from the springs of our leaders, but we also need to seek our own spring.

> She answered, "Give me a blessing; since you have given me land in the South, give me also springs of water." So he gave her the upper springs and the lower springs. (*Joshua 15:19*).

Here we see Caleb's daughter asking her father for a gift. Although she had received great amounts of land and fields, she knew that she couldn't do anything with just the land because the land is no good without water. Therefore, she asked her father for a precious gift, springs of water.

It is useless to have land, places to go, and contacts if we do not have water to give. Each one of us needs our own spring.

"Also Isaac's servants dug in the valley, and found a well of running water there." (Gen. 26:19). Isaac's servants had to dig in the valley to find a spring of living water. The action of digging demands a great amount of work, effort, and time. *This is a type of the fasted lifestyle.* If we want our own spring, we need to seek God with our whole heart digging and positioning our hearts until we find living water.

If we take a relaxed attitude, believing that someone else will find water to give us, we will never mature, nor grow, nor progress spiritually. *It is time to dig!* That is the only way we will have our own spring.

The Fruit of the First Encounter

"Then she said, 'Let me find favor in your sight, my lord; for you have comforted me, and have spoken kindly to your maidservant, though I am not like one of your maidservants' *Ruth 2:13.*

Ruth had been comforted. She no longer simply gleaned in the fields of Boaz, but she began to feel comforted by him. All the pain that Moab had caused her was finally coming to an end. The open wounds of her soul began to heal because she had found someone who spoke directly to her heart. Despite the fact that she was a foreigner, and not even one of his handmaids, Boaz's grace and love fell upon her also. *(Jer. 31:12-13).*

An encounter with Jesus causes our soul to become like a *well-watered* garden. It is He who comforts the heart and makes it rejoice. Let us not cleave to pain and sorrow, but go into His presence to be comforted, and He will speak to our heart.

Sitting At His Table

Now Boaz said to her at mealtime, "Come here, and eat of the bread, and dip your piece of bread in the vinegar." So she sat beside the reapers, and he passed parched grain to her; and she ate and was satisfied... *(Ruth 2:14).*

Things began to improve for Ruth. She was no longer just another woman who went to glean what the reapers left behind. The Master had invited her to come to his table. Do you remember who else sat at the table? Ruth had reached the same level as Lazarus. She not only worked in the fields of the lord, but was also privileged to sit at his table. What an experience this must have been for her! Ruth was surely making progress.

Knowing His Name

And her mother-in-law said to her, "Where have you gleaned today? And where did you work? Blessed be the one who took notice of you. "So she told her mother-in-law with whom she had worked, and said, "The man's name with whom I worked today is Boaz." *(Ruth 2:19)*.

The name Boaz had great significance for Ruth. What is a name? It is a term or expression that represents a person. When I mention or hear a name, this name brings to mind that person, what I know about him, and the impression that he has left. For example, I can know the name of the president of my country, but really all I know about him is what the press has said. I know his name, but I have not had a personal experience with him; I do not know him intimately. I have never seen him in person, and I certainly have never sat down at the table with him. Nevertheless, if you would ask me what his name is, I could tell you. This was not the case with Ruth. She had seen Boaz, personally heard his voice, and ate with him at his table. When Ruth said Boaz's name, the memories of her experiences and encounters with him came to mind.

The name of God speaks about His nature and His personality — who He really is. The memories of our encounters with Him come to mind when we mention His name. *"And those who know Your name will put their trust in You"* (Ps. 9:10).

The Guidance of the Spirit

And Naomi said to Ruth her daughter-in-law, "It is good, my daughter, that you go out with his young women, and that people do not meet you in any other field." -*Ruth 2:22*.

Guidance — That's what Ruth needed to go deeper in her relationship with Boaz. So, *Naomi* speaks out with wisdom from above. In this period of her life, Naomi is a poetic parallel to the *Holy Spirit*. She began to give testimony in favor of Boaz, telling Ruth that it was best for her to stay with Boaz's maidens and that they not find her in any other field. Naomi began to guide Ruth, telling her what was best for her. The Holy Spirit always gives testimony of Jesus, and guides us in the whole truth (*Jn 15:26; 16:13-14*).

Ruth obeyed *Naomi* and worked alongside the handmaidens of Boaz for the remainder of the harvest. Ruth's greatest achievement at this point was to work in the fields of Boaz. Surely, she continued to eat at his table, but *there was more than this*.

The Preparation

Naomi was not content with the fact that the relationship between *Boaz* and *Ruth* consisted solely of eating together.

Then Naomi her mother-in-law said to her, "My daughter, shall I not seek security for you, that it may be well with you? Now Boaz, whose young women you were with, is he not our relative? In fact, he is winnowing barley tonight at the threshing floor. Therefore **wash yourself and anoint yourself, put on your best garment** and go down to the threshing floor; but do not make yourself known to the man until he has finished eating and drinking. Then....when he lies down, that you shall notice the place where he lies; and you shall go in, **uncover his feet,** and lie down; and he will tell you what you should do *(Ruth 3:1-4).*

Naomi showed Ruth the way to enter into a more intimate relationship with Boaz. She directed Ruth to the dwelling of Boaz, and specified to her how she should prepare herself to go *(Ruth 3:3).*

> ➢ First of all, Ruth could not present herself dirty. *She had to wash and clean herself.* The action of washing speaks of purity and holiness. This flows out of a right understanding of the work of Calvary.
> ➢ Then *she had to anoint herself* with perfume. I believe that this perfume speaks of extravagant worship.
> ➢ After that, she had to clothe herself. *(Let your garments always be white, and let your head lack no oil. Eccl. 9:8).* The garment represents the righteousness of Christ.

It is as if *Naomi* told Ruth: *"Look, you can't present yourself before Boaz like that. We aren't talking about going out to glean, what you are going to be doing is getting to know him more intimately and allowing him to get to know you."*

In the book of Song of Songs, Solomon describes what the preparation of the *Bride* produces in the *Bridegroom:*

"How fair is your love, My sister, my spouse! How much better than wine is your love, and the scent of your perfumes than all spices! Your lips, O my spouse, drip as the honeycomb; Honey and milk are under your tongue; and the fragrance of your garments is like the fragrance of Lebanon" (Sg. 4:10-11)

The Obedience to the Spirit

> And she said to her, "All that you say to me I will do." So she went down to the threshing floor and did according to all that her mother-in-law instructed her *(Ruth 3:5-6).*

If Ruth hadn't obeyed *Naomi*, she never would have become the wife of Boaz. Ruth could have easily rebelled against Naomi's advice. Nevertheless, she chose to obey.

The *Holy Spirit* will show us the way, but He will not force us to walk in it. It is necessary that we willingly obey Him, despite the fact that we have a free will. If we choose to disobey the advice of the Spirit, we should keep in mind the following: He is the one who knows the depth of God, and if we don't obey Him, we will always remain on the surface. *(1Cor. 2:10-11; 1Thess. 5:19).*

At The Feet of Boaz

> Now it happened at midnight that the man was startled, and turned himself; and there, a woman was lying at his feet. And he said, "Who are you?" So she answered, "I am Ruth, your maidservant. Take your maidservant under your wing, for you are a close relative." *(Ruth 3:8-9).*

In the customs of this time, that action of Ruth lying at the feet of Boaz transmitted her desire for him to marry her.

Even the phrase, *"Take your maidservant under your wing"* expresses her desire to be his wife. God Himself uses this phrase in reference to Jerusalem: *"When I passed by you again and looked upon you, indeed your time was the time of love; so I spread My wing over you and covered your nakedness. Yes, I swore an oath to you and entered into a covenant with you, and you became Mine," says the Lord God" (Ez. 16:8).*

It was as if Ruth had said to Boaz: *"Look, you know that I am your servant, but I am not satisfied just working in your fields, nor am I satisfied eating at your table. I want more! I desire to know you intimately. Take me under your wing."*

And Boaz responded: *"Blessed are you of the Lord, my daughter! For you have shown more kindness at the end than at the beginning, in that you did not go after young men, whether poor or rich." (Ruth 3:10).* Ruth had not gone out seeking young men. What did the young men mean to her? The lusts of the flesh, something that Ruth may have liked to experience because she was also young. *Nevertheless*, she chose Boaz, being older than her. Ruth died to the desires of her *flesh* in order to fulfill those of the *Spirit* because there was something in Boaz that fascinated and captivated her heart, something that could not compare to the pleasures of this life. They were eternal, everlasting, and she wanted to have him forever.

"And now, my daughter, do not fear. I will do for you all that you request, for all the people of my town know that you are a virtuous woman." (Ruth 3:11).

The relationship between Ruth and Boaz had definitely changed. She stirred the fire of his heart. The words that Boaz spoke here are similar to those that Moses heard: *"So the Lord said to Moses, "I will also do this thing that you have spoken; for you have found grace in My sight, and I know you by name." (Ex. 33:17).*

Being at the feet of Boaz did not only meant that Ruth was getting to know him, but he was also getting to know her.

Isn't it interesting to see the place that Ruth was guided to? Isn't it the same place where Mary of Bethany came to know Jesus more intimately? Of course it is. And it is to this place that the Holy Spirit wants to take us — *to Jesus' feet.*

Listen to me, O royal daughter; take to heart what I say. Forget your people and your homeland far away. For your royal husband delights in your beauty; honor him, for he is your lord. *(Ps. 45:10-11, NLT).*

The Ministry Of Life

So Boaz took Ruth and she became his wife; and when he went in to her, the Lord gave her conception, and she bore a son… gave him a name, saying, "There is a son born to Naomi." And they called his name Obed. He is the father of Jesse, the father of David *(Ruth 4:13, 17).*

There were more than words exchanged between Ruth and Boaz. *Obed* was not the fruit of sporadic conversation. Ruth did not conceive by simply being close to Boaz, nor by just receiving his caresses. The phrase *"and he went in to her,"* indicates that Boaz did more than touch Ruth. There was an intimate exchange between them.

Please hear with your spiritual ears. Many people are satisfied with just a touch of Jesus, or hearing His voice from time to time, (and this is wonderful). Tremendous as it is, it's not enough. One touch of Jesus blesses us… an intimate and continuous relationship with Him changes us constantly and forever.

In these last two chapters I have tried to focus on the importance of growing in intimacy with the Lord. Do you know why? Because if we don't grow in intimacy with the Jesus, we will not be able to conceive, nor give birth. In other words, we will not bring life into this world, only programs and religious forms.

Let's discover Jesus' feet... the favorite place of a prophetic worshiper. There, His magnificent beauty will fascinate our hearts and will affect our music, our worship, and our entire lives.

- To Meditate -

✓ Getting to know Jesus is a process. As we live and walk with Him, the Holy Spirit will expand and enlarge our understanding of His person and how important we are to Him.

✓ The kingdom of God is full of blessings. Everything that we need is there. *On the other hand*, it is interesting to see that we can have the blessings of the kingdom without knowing the King.

✓ One touch of Jesus blesses us. An intimate and continuous relationship with Him changes us constantly and forever.

✓ Let's discover Jesus' feet — the favorite place of a prophetic worshiper. There, His magnificent beauty will fascinate our hearts and will affect our music, our worship, and our entire lives.

-Recommended Resources-

MAJESTIC SPLENDOR

A new worship release from Pablo Perez. **Majestic Splendor** is a collection of songs filled with passion and longing for the Lord. The devotional lyrics and soaring music will lead your heart into the throne room of God.

INTERCESSORY WORSHIP

This project is a compilation of powerful and anointed *Harp & Bowl* sessions. In *Intercessory Worship*, several apostolic prayers and hymns from the book of Revelation are covered. The combination of worship and intercession is clearly demonstrated in this CD.

www.jasperstonemusic.com

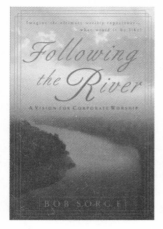

FOLLOWING THE RIVER

Imagine the ultimate worship experience — what would it be like? Using a sound scriptural foundation, Bob paints a vivid picture of what corporate worship can become. Get a glimpse of where God is taking us. There is a sweep-you-off-your-feet depth to the river of God's delights that is more than possible, it is inevitable!

AFTER GOD'S OWN HEART

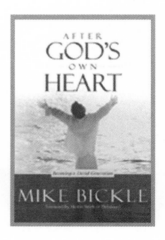

One of Mike Bickle's best books. You can become a student of God's emotions and learn how godly commitment and obedience help you form a mature love. It s time for you to develop a heart that is anchored and sustained by an outrageous love that comes only from Him. Experience a transition that gives you a new passion, resulting in the fulfillment of God's promises.

COME TO PAPA

Come To Papa by Gary Wiens is a collection of meditations on the nature of God the Father as revealed through the teachings of Jesus in the New Testament. It is written in the hope of bringing healing to those with distorted images of God as Father, so that many will turn to Him to find hope in increasingly desperate times.

www.fotb.com

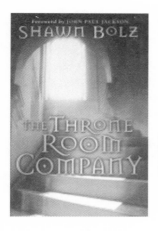

THE THRONE ROOM COMPANY

Thought provoking and profoundly perceptive, The Throne Room Company has the power to revolutionize your understanding of God. In this book, Shawn Bolz reveals a fascinating message from Heaven that will penetrate the deep places of your heart. His stories and wisdom will guide you to a more noble place.

ENJOYING GOD

This book by S. J. Hill will open your heart to the revelation of God as your Father. It will also expose misconceptions you may have had about His personality that have hindered you from growing in your relationship with Him. *Enjoying God* will move you from duty to delight in your relationship with Christ.

PLEASURES EVERMORE

In this compelling and highly readable book, Sam Storms presents a fresh and liberating perspective on why a relationship with God is not only possible but irresistibly pleasurable. Once you discover that God delights in your company, your desire for Him will only be satisfied by drawing closer to His unquenchable love through a life of passionate service.

www.fotb.com

-To be released in 2005-

another book from Pablo Pérez

Bridal Worship — The response of a lovesick heart, a heart that has been fascinated by the beauty of God.

Bridal worship is the response of a soul that has been ruined by encountering the love of His heavenly Bridegroom. It is a passionate demonstration of love and desire, an intimate expression that reflects the reality of eternal and superior pleasures.

Bridal worship is the sweet aroma that comes from the church at the end of the age. A beautiful and costly fragrance that ignites the end-time revival and releases the fiery zeal of God's affections across the nations.

Bridal worship will fuel the prayer movement around the globe, unveiling a level of intimacy that we have not yet known and leaving millions of souls lovesick for the Man Christ Jesus.